Report Card

The Weekly Education of a School Board Member

James Patrick Hussey

A SCARECROWEDUCATION BOOK

The Scarecrow Press, Inc.
Lanham, Maryland, Toronto, and Oxford
2003

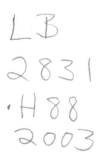

LB
2831
.H88
2003

Published in the United States of America
by ScarecrowEducation
An imprint of The Rowman & Littlefield Publishing Group, Inc.
4501 Forbes Boulevard, Suite 200, Lanham, MD 20706
www.scarecroweducation.com

PO Box 317
Oxford
OX2 9RU, UK

British Library Cataloguing in Publication Information Available

Library of Congress Cataloging-in-Publication Data
Hussey, James Patrick, 1960–
  Report card : the weekly education of a school board member / James
Patrick Hussey.   p. cm.
  "A ScarecrowEducation book."
  ISBN 1-57886-023-7 (pbk. : alk. paper)
  1. School boards—United States—Anecdotes. 2. School board members—
United States—Anecdotes. 3. School management and organization—United
States—Anecdotes. I. Title.
LB2831.H88 2003
379.1'531—dc21   200300824

∞™ The paper used in this publication meets the minimum requirements of
American National Standard for Information Sciences—Permanence of
Paper for Printed Library Materials, ANSI/NISO Z39.48-1992.
Manufactured in the United States of America.

To my wife, children, and parents for their uncommon patience and support.

And to my high school teachers, especially Madame Jacobsen, who taught me French (and English); Mr. Kanellis, who believed in enjoying an argument; Mr. Van Zante, who insisted his students write the truth; and Mr. Barker, who let his teachers do their jobs.

"Men occasionally stumble over the truth, but most of them pick themselves up and hurry off as if nothing had happened."
—Winston Churchill, world leader

"I know you're making a difference, because everybody is complaining about you."
—Bob Lutz, auto executive

"What's another word for thesaurus?"
—Steven Wright, comedian

Contents

Introduction

School board members may be among the last "pure" public servants left in America. In Iowa, we receive zero pay, little recognition and our share of grief, yet our nation's future might rest as much on our shoulders as it does on our more celebrated political peers.

Whether we come to our boards as farmers, physicians or "intellectual freedom fighters," we share the same basic job description—to create educational environments where students can mature into contributing members of society.

Long before I was elected to the Mid-Prairie Community School District Board of Directors, I grew up in Iowa City, the school district immediately to the north, graduating in 1978. During the intervening decades, I studied across the Midwest before heading to Alaska for 13 years, where I worked as a reporter, journalism professor and educational administrator—and married and had two children, with whom I returned to Iowa in 1996.

K–12 education had changed during my absence. No longer could schools simply open their doors and expect students, staff and stacks of dollar bills to stream their way. Parents and taxpayers demanded accountability, "excellence" and even entrepreneurship. As a community member with a personal interest in outstanding schools, I figured if I didn't want to shut up, I needed to put up—and ran for Mid-Prairie's board in 1999.

I soon found myself on the business side of the board table. To communicate our goals, my colleagues and I decided to write a weekly newspaper column, the *Report Card*, that our two local newspapers, the *Kalona News* and the *Wellman Advance,* graciously agreed to publish.

I wrote the first article, the second—and ultimately 100 more.

In keeping with our agricultural heritage, I regarded the columns as seeds planted in hope of future harvests, rather than instruments of immediate advocacy (although some, I suspect, thought of them more as "fertilizer"). I also tried to make the *Report Card* fun. My best teachers always took their subjects seriously, but rarely themselves.

Finally, since public service becomes less so once you start skimming off the top, should this book have the good fortune to make any money, 100 percent of my profits will be redirected to education-related charities, specifically:

- Mid-Prairie programs that develop and celebrate the unique gifts of each of its students
- The Kalona Library Foundation, in support of lifelong learning
- The Prevcil School of Music, in recognition of the role the fine arts play in a well-rounded education
- Richmond, Iowa's Holy Trinity Catholic Church's religious education program, because none of us has all the answers

My hope is *Report Card* will prove interesting, and occasionally inspiring, to teachers, administrators, students of educational leadership, elected officials, and all those who love learning—especially those who serve on America's boards of education.

The next two hundred pages are filled with my observations and ideas, which you are free to take or leave as you please. If you care enough to read, think and especially *act* upon your considered opinions as a result, I will consider this effort an unqualified success.

Chapter One

Philosophy

WHEN I WAS FOUR

Four-year-old children are joys to behold. They're too young to have
  learned it's best not to be bold.
They'll draw lions and tigers, giraffes and wombats. It wouldn't cross
  their minds to say, "I can't do that."

But when they turn five, a terrible thing happens. They quit having
  fun and start going to classes.
We sit them up straight and make them write using D'Nelian, turning
  them into tiny chameleons.

We mold them, we shape them, of this there's no bones. We're proud
  of the way we churn out little clones.
Our best we honor and send on to college, where their heads get
  stuffed with more useless knowledge.

Somehow it seems more than a little absurd, to think there's more
  truth in a book than in the song of a bird.
If I were in charge, what would I stress? First, I'd toss out the worksheets with the standardized tests.

I'd close Little League and let kids play their own games, with their
  own sets of rules called by their own goofy names.
Kids would eat many more pizzas and many less livers, and for every
  textbook they'd study, they'd read one or more rivers.

As they grew older they'd give up life on the run, and practice the
   good things—like a snooze in the sun.
They would devote much more effort to paddling canoes, and skip all
   those board meetings crunching cashews.

We spend too much time counting money and calories, judging ourselves by our waistlines and salaries.
When we leave this world we're going to be dead, so why not depart
   it well-rounded instead of well-read?

Let's spend more time laughing, less time keeping score, and start living our lives like when we were four.
When we rise above society's lies, it's then we'll be educated and indeed truly wise.

SLAVES TO EDUCATIONAL ABUNDANCE

What can you get for $14 these days? In my school district, you can buy
a half-day's instruction for our average child. In other parts of the world,
$14 can buy a whole child—forever.

As this is being written, authorities are searching for a ship carrying as
many as 180 child slaves. In West Africa, 200,000 children may be involved in involuntary servitude. According to the American Anti-Slavery
Group, as many as 10 million children worldwide may be caught up in the
modern slave trade.

What do these horrific statistics have to do with the students in your
schools? Like a two-by-four across the forehead, they should remind us of
our remarkable good fortune to be living in America, and from an academic perspective, the children these numbers represent should compel us
to make the most of our extraordinary educational privileges.

Look in the mirror. It's been a while, but I clearly recall suffering from
"senioritis" before graduating from high school. Once I had compiled the
credits required for my diploma, I coasted. I kept up my grades, but in a
schedule that was measurably less demanding than before.

While I risk sounding like the father who orders his kids to eat "because
there are children starving in China," I cannot excuse my sloth. Throughout
history, few children have enjoyed the advantage of being taught by caring

adults inside warm classrooms and with full stomachs. Now that I'm older, I realize not making the most of that chance was nothing less than shameful.

Similarly, I once had a teaching colleague who was infamous for slapping in videotapes whenever it was too hard or inconvenient to come up with suitable lectures or scientific experiments. His students didn't complain, because as long as they watched TV, they'd pass their tests. Did they make the most of their time in that classroom? From what I hear, they did not. Wasting the learning time of an entire classroom of students only multiplies the sin.

Unlike the children on the slave ship, Americans live under the illusion of unlimited educational opportunity—and for good reason. While the world's least-advantaged youngsters can only dream of going to school, our kids are legally required to attend classes.

In most of the world, college educations are available only to the brightest students from the most affluent families. In contrast, virtually any American who wants a higher education can get one.

My local community college, for example, declares its "open admission policy reflects our commitment to bringing cultural, occupational and educational opportunities within the reach of everyone." The *American Heritage Dictionary*, in turn, defines *open admissions* as "a policy that permits enrollment of a student in a college or university without regard to academic qualifications."

While I strongly support both compulsory attendance and the community college mission, I have a nagging suspicion our educational abundance somehow undermines our appreciation, and even respect, for learning itself.

Why exert yourself as a senior, if you know you'll "earn" a diploma for a half-hearted effort? Why study, if you know you have an easy grader for a teacher? Why put in the time to prepare for postsecondary studies, when you know you can be admitted "without regard to academic achievement"?

The answer to those questions can be found on the slave ship. As a child, I believed I had time to waste as it suited me. I now realize the most long-lived among us will be on this planet for an instant, and that time itself is the ultimate scarce commodity.

We may think we can "catch up later," but the clock ticks in only one direction. What we should think about are the children on the slave ship, and the $14 it took to get them there, the next time we are tempted to blow off a class, coast through a semester, slap in a videotape, or do anything else that dishonors the precious educational opportunities we have been afforded.

The kids on that ship wouldn't take those gifts for granted, and neither should we.

GENERALISSIMO OF MUD AND MAYHEM

Bill Watterson—creator of the comic strip *Calvin and Hobbes*—is my family's favorite author. Since our children entered school, we have read virtually every night about Calvin, a precocious 1st-grader with too much imagination for his own good, and Hobbes, the stuffed tiger with whom he shares his skewed views of life.

What's especially appealing about Calvin is that he doesn't like organized anything. His favorite sport is "Calvinball," whose only rule is "there are no rules." Through our readings, I hope to nurture a healthy disrespect for mindless conformity and to teach our kids that the best times are often those when there's "nothing to do."

Like many modern parents, though, I talk a better game than I walk.

During my childhood, I played one instrument (string bass), participated on one team (debate), and had paper routes. That's pretty much it for extracurricular commitments. During my downtime, I biked hundreds of miles, walked in the woods with my dog, fished every farm pond within cycling distance, and filled countless hours with the unscripted adventures of youth.

My ten-year-old son Patrick, on the other hand, juggles three instruments and the attendant lessons and rehearsals, squeezing in dance and Chinese on the weekends. Nine-year-old Molly is just one instrument behind, and is anxiously awaiting 5th grade so she can start the flute.

Occasionally, Patrick or Molly will grumble about their schedules—but after each "event," second thoughts seem to vanish. While they're forsaking T-ball this summer, they're insisting on soccer and swimming lessons. In the meantime, they're off to lessons three to five days a week, not counting the five days they spend in the 5th and 3rd grades, respectively.

If that sounds like more than a seven-day week, believe me, my wife, Jean, and I know. I hesitate to even think about high school, when homework and after-school activities really kick into gear.

Is this crazy, or what? According to *Newsweek*, if the Husseys are nuts, we're not alone.

Newsweek suggests too many parents are reading about Tiger Woods, and figure if their kids aren't excelling at an early age, they'll never catch up. According to Stanford's William Damon, "I think parents have a sense we've become a 'winner takes all' society . . . and if you miss the top rung, you sink down into hardship and discomfort."

Adds *Newsweek*, "What families risk losing in this insane frenzy . . . is the soul of childhood and the joy of family life. 'These are supposed to be the years that kids wander and pal around, without being faced with the pressures of the real world,' says Damon. Instead, 'the parenting experience is being ruined. . . . It's all about how to get into Yale.'"

You might think this is an issue for only big-city parents of big-headed children. However, right now in our state legislature, there are rumblings that we need to set one night each week legally off-limits to school activities, with the hope our youngsters will have shots at the childhoods most of us enjoyed.

We've already laid down the law—sort of—in our house. The sooner everyone finishes their obligations, the more "fun" we can have. For example, if the kids are ready for bed by 9 p.m., they get 10 pages of *Calvin and Hobbes*. If it's 9:30 p.m., they get four, and if it's past 10 p.m., they get zero—unless I'm feeling charitable.

Recently, there have been too many nights without readings. Our overcrowded schedules also meant Patrick and Molly didn't have time for the kind of experiences Calvin described to his father one "usual" summer day: "I am the Downhill Tumble-and-Roll Champ, King of the Toad Finders, Captain of the High-Altitude Tree Branch Vista Club, second-place finisher in the 'Round-the-Yard-Backward Dash, Premier Burper State Division, Sodbuster and Worm Scout First Order, and Generalissimo of the Mud-and-Mayhem Society."

Now that's a day.

With the best intentions, our school district provides students 180 days of classroom learning each year, hundreds more hours of homework, and myriad other activities to help them make the most of each waking moment.

However, in our pell-mell efforts to excel at everything, I hope we—as parents and as schools—never forget to teach our kids to seek out, as Calvin does, the adventures available to each of us during our everyday, "ordinary" lives.

THE NAIL THAT STICKS OUT

In Japan, every toddler is taught, "The nail that sticks out gets hammered down." The lesson isn't about carpentry, but culture. In contrast to America, where we claim to revere individual achievement, in Asia, conformity is often the higher ideal.

According to Yukio Noguchi of Tokyo University, "Respect for authority and structure is inculcated in children from preschool. The shame of being different is emphasized. Making no mistakes and no real contribution is much better than failing by trying something new."

Of course, Americans have different value systems from those found in the Orient—or do we? Each fall, our school district measures its kids with standardized tests, which we use to compare ourselves with schools statewide. Our state then ranks itself against national norms, and finally, our nation weighs its achievements against countries worldwide—including Japan.

It's not bad to know where we stand, and it's OK to insist that our children master basic academic skills. However, if we mindlessly comply with the MBA's mantra, "What gets measured gets done," we risk forgetting what learning should be all about—the exploration of new ideas.

Albert Einstein revolutionized our understanding of the universe, but quit physics for a year after being forced to cram for an exam. Einstein wrote, "It is a grave mistake to think the enjoyment of seeing and searching can be promoted by means of coercion and a sense of duty."

Few of us are Einsteins, but think back on your schooling. Did its most meaningful moments involve memorizing multiplication tables or plowing through piles of homework?

Of course not. They came when you exceeded the expectations of your teachers, your parents and even yourself. While competence is easily calculated, passion is harder to appraise—but in the long run, it's what changes our lives and the world in which we live.

Unfortunately, the creative flame is easily extinguished. In one study, Harvard's Teresa Amabile had two groups of children create paintings and then collages. The first group finished painting and then immediately started their collages. Group Two had their paintings evaluated before beginning their second projects.

Artists who reviewed the work found the collages from unevaluated children "were markedly more creative than the collages coming from the evaluated group." Anticipating judgment, the evaluated students pulled their punches to avoid making "mistakes"—at the cost of real creativity.

To protect creative passions, Amabile recommends that parents spontaneously celebrate outstanding report cards, rather than offer "Pay for an A" performance plans. She says parents should emphasize values over rules, and create homes "where you and your children habitually try to do things in new, interesting ways."

Sadly, by the time most of us become parents, the words *new* and *interesting* have long been purged from our vocabularies. Consider, for example, two hypothetical job applicants, one a "safe" choice and the other a "stretch." Whom would YOU hire?

According to consultant and author Tom Peters, "We hire that kid who never missed a day of kindergarten, who never got a word wrong on a spelling test, who had a 4.0 average in high school, and who comes to the interview without a single hair out of place.

"I'll tell you who I want to hire. I want the woman . . . who took off for two years. There was a chance that she was working for Mother Teresa. Maybe she was knocking off 7-Elevens. We don't know, but at least once in her life she had the guts to thumb her nose at the establishment. If we have the guts to hire her, then maybe it will happen a second time."

Of course, schools—from preschool to the postsecondary level—tend to be designed to punish, or at least discourage, rule-breakers. What probably gets discouraged after a decade or more of absorbing the culture is the willingness to take real risks and intellectual leaps of faith. As a result, our honor rolls tend to be crammed with well-mannered students who churn out "safe," capable work. Our society needs to find a middle ground in which classroom competence is quantified, but also one in which impassioned excellence—at whatever level a child is capable of—is actively encouraged.

S. I. Hayakawa, a college president who later became a California senator, once wrote, "If you see in any given situation only what everybody else can see, you (are less) a representative of your culture than you are a victim of it."

Hayakawa, a product of Asian parents and the North American educational system, hit the nail right on the head.

IOWA'S EDUCATION PRESIDENT

Every four years, Iowans meet with neighbors and friends in hundreds of schools, libraries and meeting halls across our state in our fabled presidential caucuses. Just about as many reporters traipse in from all corners of the world to watch us do it.

While the itinerant media horde follow those who might be president, documenting their every handshake, gaffe and pratfall, few scribes write stories about the one man from Iowa who actually became president—Herbert Clark Hoover.

Hoover isn't listed in the pantheon of great presidents by most historians, or even by many Iowans. Until the past few years, I shared the same opinion, but as a would-be lifelong learner, I'm getting smarter.

Orphaned in early childhood, Hoover was making more money than any man his age in the world by the age of 28. Instead of idly counting his cash, Hoover volunteered to lead relief efforts that saved millions of lives across Europe and Asia, a fact forgotten by most of us. And while Hoover had the bad luck to settle in at the White House at the same time the United States' economic bubble burst, he also took advantage of his time as president to promote our nation's most important industry and its most precious products—our educational system and our children.

Hoover, a Republican, sounded like anything but a curmudgeonly conservative when his *Children's Charter* called "For every child a school which is safe from hazards, sanitary, properly equipped, lighted, and ventilated." The charter, a product of *President Hoover's White House Conference on Child Health and Protection*, recognized "the rights of the child as the first rights of citizenship."

Hoover believed our future success as a nation depended upon our current investment in children. While his left-leaning words may have gotten him hooted out of contemporary candidate debates, Hoover said in the 1930s that every child deserved "a community which recognizes and plans for his needs, protects him against physical dangers, moral hazards, and disease; provides him with safe and wholesome places for play and recreation; and makes provision for his cultural and social needs."

Hoover's attitudes were no doubt shaped by his own difficult childhood. Despite his humble origins, and even though it might have served him well in politics, Hoover never claimed to be a "Common Man" and, in fact, detested the label. According to Hoover, "We are in danger of developing a cult of the Common Man, which means a cult of mediocrity. But there is at least one hopeful sign: I have never been able to find out who this Common Man is. In fact, most Americans, and especially women, will get mad and fight if you try calling them common."

According to Hoover, the recipe for uncommon Americans was education, specifically "teaching and training as will prepare him for successful parenthood, homemaking, and the rights of citizenship." As a boy who grew up poor on a featureless prairie, on the "West Branch" of a river that is really more of a creek, Hoover made a particular point of demanding, "For every rural child as satisfactory schooling and health services as for the city child, and an extension to rural families of social, recreational and cultural facilities."

The notion that we should commonly commit to developing uncommon citizens is too rarely voiced in today's politics. Most candidates run for office scared to death of being tarred with the "liberal" label, which the term *common commitment* seems to suggest. At the same time, no matter how much power and wealth they may bring to the political arena, our citizen-candidates do their best to convince us they're just plain folks.

Hoover would have none of it. He reminded us, "The great human advances have not been brought about by mediocre men and women. They were brought about by distinctly uncommon people with vital sparks of leadership." Hoover further noted, "It is a curious fact that when you are sick you want an uncommon doctor; if your car breaks down you want an uncommonly good mechanic; when we get into war we want dreadfully an uncommon admiral and an uncommon general."

Each four years, as the political spotlight shines briefly on Iowa, it is a good time for all Americans to remember our 31st president—a good man who deserves more credit than he generally receives. While others have laid claim to the title "Education President," Herbert Hoover gets my vote. In his words, "I have never met a father and mother who did not want their children to grow up to be uncommon men and women. May it always be so. For the future of America rests not in mediocrity, but in the constant renewal of leadership in every phase of our national life."

BRAINS SECOND TO NUNS

As I write, I am two hours removed from having my bones rattled by a rousing rendition of the *Mid-Prairie Fight Song*. A "Monster Band" of more than 200 Golden Hawks, ranging from "enthusiastic" 5th graders to polished high schoolers, will shake the walls with an impossible-to-ignore display of passion for their music and schools.

For some, the enthusiasm will be short-lived. Whether it's in the transition to middle school or to "real life," their instruments will eventually be sold or stored in the attic. For others, though, music will be a lifelong love—and a growing body of evidence suggests such zeal not only makes lives longer, but more worth living.

Unfortunately, passions cannot be programmed—despite the wishes of adults. For example, most parents have heard of the Mozart Effect, which suggests that exposing infants to Mozart's melodies might cause his genius to wear off on kids' growing brains.

My wife and I mixed Mozart and Motown CDs at our babies' bedsides, but according to a Harvard analysis of 50 years of "Mozart" research, there is no evidence kids derive any long-term benefit from such musical manipulation. So much for our efforts, much less those of mothers who strapped on "pregaphones" to bombard their babies with music in the womb.

Such actions reflect a desire to be good parents, but according to the *Time* story, "So You Want to Raise a Superkid," parents desperate to boost their babies' brainpower often have the opposite effect. By kindergarten, "the brains of stressed out kids can start to look an awful lot like the brains of stressed adults, with increased levels of adrenaline and cortisol. . . . Keep the brain on edge long enough, and the changes become long-lasting, making learning harder as kids get older."

Does that mean you simply let nature take its course? Alas, passivity is also the wrong answer. While Mozart may not make a difference to the diapered set, the deficits we accumulate in elementary school often express themselves as we grow older.

The most compelling evidence comes from convents. The 678 participants in the recently published *Nun Study*, who range in age from 75 to 106, participate in annual examinations to compare their current mental and physical functioning with the eloquence of autobiographical essays they wrote a half-century, or longer, ago.

Those who expressed themselves best in their 20s had far higher chances of avoiding dementia in their 70s, 80s and beyond. Speaking to *USA Today*, author David Snowdon said, "Aging is overrated. . . .You've got to develop your mind to its highest potential in young life, and as an adult, you've got to keep that and train the mind to its highest function."

The nuns are not only studied in life, but in death. Since the research began, 335 nuns have died. Postmortem analyses show that even though half had conditions that would normally create dementia, many showed few signs of impairment during life. One nun could out-argue Snowdon, but upon her death, was found to have a brain riddled with the tangled proteins that characterize Alzheimer's disease. Again, "Those who are hopeful, happy and optimistic live much longer. That happy state is also a healthy state."

One final study: Donald Redelmeier had the inspired idea to compare 762 actors and actresses, some who had won Oscars and others who had only been nominated. The two groups generally came from the same socioeconomic background, and shared the same privileged gene pool. He found winners lived an average of four years longer than the nominees did, and multiple-Oscar-winners lived six years longer.

The results suggest that if average folks could internalize the sense of peace and accomplishment of the Oscar winners, who found their passions ratified beyond doubt (remember Sally Field? "You like me! You really like me!"), they too could live longer and healthier lives. Redelmeier contends, "Parents, teachers, politicians and the media who have the power to honor and acknowledge social worth might keep this in mind."

That brings us back to the Mid-Prairie Monster Band. Some students in the band will uncover their enthusiasms through music, and others through careers in medicine or mathematics, or as moms. Tragically, some may never discover what makes their souls sing, and may live shorter, sicker and sadder lives because of it.

If we can provide our kids ample opportunities to uncover and act upon their lives' passions, then we'll have truly provided educations that last a lifetime.

KEEPING IT CORE

Another high school class has graduated. Ready or not, the 81 students who received diplomas in our gym last Sunday are beginning the next stage of their lives. While I hope our graduates remember the formal lessons we taught in our schools, I would rejoice if they took a moment to note—in writing—what they care most about in life as they officially advance from adolescence to adulthood, and remember to pull out the list every few years to see if they're "keeping it core."

At the risk of appearing not "hep," if I understand adolescent argot, "keeping it core" means staying true to yourself—not twisting your values to meet social expectations. From a fashion perspective, wearing no-name jeans is "core." Donning designer duds because glossy ads tell you to makes you a "wannabe," along with other slang terms best left in the school yard.

High school was the last time many of us had the freedom—or the courage—to stay core. Unlike the "real world," we weren't forced to choose between nourishing our souls and feeding our families. We took the classes we wanted, cut our hair (when some of us still had it) as we pleased, and our dreams were limited only by our imaginations. We lived by the credo of the ultimate "core" philosopher, Henry David Thoreau, who counseled, "Distrust any enterprise that requires new clothes."

Nearly 200 years later, David Brooks shares Thoreau's doubts, and has written "The Organization Kid," this year's most influential article on education. Published in *The Atlantic*, Brooks asserts the "problem" with too many of today's kids is that they're everything we want them to be.

"The world they live in seems fundamentally just. If you work hard, behave pleasantly, explore your interests, volunteer your time, obey the codes of political correctness, and take the right pills to balance your brain chemistry, you will be rewarded with a wonderful ascent in the social hierarchy," writes Brooks. "There is a fundamental order to the universe, and it works. If you play by its rules and defer to its requirements, you will lead a pretty fantastic life."

Brooks objects to the complacency bred by a culture in which everyone understands, and obeys, the rules. Conformity, he contends, makes for pleasant lives—just not great ones.

"These young people are wonderful to be around; if they are indeed running the country in a few decades, we'll be in fine shape," says Brooks. "All this ambition and aspiration is looking for new tests to ace, new clubs to be president of, new services to perform, but finding that none of these challenges is the ultimate challenge, and none of the rewards is the ultimate reward."

What is the ultimate reward? Staying in the earthly realm, it means dancing to one's own tunes, rather than spinning to society's gyroscope. That's why, while memories are still fresh, this year's graduates should jot down what makes their hearts race—and why all of us should take advantage of the commencement season to dust off any long-shelved dreams from our youths.

A quarter-century ago, I loved debate, journalism and playing the string bass. As part of my own self-improvement, I am trying to rebuild some of my core the years have eroded beyond easy recognition. This column, in fact, is a twofer: it presents one side of a debate (success vs. "success"), and it does so in a journalistic forum. As far as the bass goes, I haven't played a song since 1978, but before this year is out, I'm determined to set the neighbors' dogs howling by picking up the big fiddle again.

The night of this writing, I attended Senior Class Night, in which our graduates hauled in 49 separate awards and scholarships. Our seniors should be pleased with their efforts, and our community should be just as proud of its support for education.

Our graduates will eventually discover that external rewards become fewer and farther in between, but they should never become discouraged by that reality. While our society does its best to reinforce uniformity, if our seniors succeed in "keeping it core," they'll discover life's rewards are nearly limitless—and provide great examples for their elders, as we try to emulate the enthusiasm for life embodied in this year's graduating class.

WHO SAID LIFE WAS FAIR?

When I left Iowa in 1978, I didn't know a soul at Macalester College, the school I was to attend in St. Paul, Minnesota. So, when asked my preferences regarding a roommate, I requested an international roommate if one might be available.

One was. Greeting me my first day at Mac was Abdulreza Saadat. While Reza was adjusting to his first Minnesota winter, halfway around the world in Iran his family and friends were coping with the overthrow of the shah, and the imposition of strict rules governing public and private life by the Ayatollah Khomeini.

A year later, when U.S. hostages were seized in Tehran, many Americans tossed all Iranians into the same pot, hating them as much as we suspected they hated us. Because of Reza, though, I knew many Iranian men wanted the same things for their lives that American men wanted for ours—satisfying careers, happy families, and—ayatollahs or not—opportunities to listen to good music and enjoy the company of pretty girls.

While our public schools are rightfully judged by how well they teach students to read and write, perhaps their most underappreciated function is that they force people from different backgrounds to get along. If you're a local resident, your kids have the right to attend the local public schools— no matter what your creed, nationality or socioeconomic background, and no matter who might not like it.

While private schools, like Macalester, have their place, it is often only in our "come one, come all" public schools that diverse populations are forced to study, play and coexist together in some degree of harmony.

Toward that end, it is foolish to say that had the September 11 terrorists had American friends growing up, the atrocities they visited upon us would have never happened. Still, I can't help but believe that had they truly known more of us, they might have more successfully resisted the murderous message that's resulted in so much sorrow.

The Public Education Network, an advocacy group, wrote after the attacks, "Public schools are the institutions in most communities where common values are expressed, shared, and taught. Strong public schools . . . are an important line of defense against ignorance, hatred, and intolerance."

More than our bombs, the patrons of terror fear our values. They understand that over time, the free-flowing water of liberty will erode the hardest rocks of hatred and intolerance.

Later in my college career, I had roommates from Iraq and Sudan, nations also linked to terror. While my modest contacts obviously weren't enough to turn their national leaders around, I'm confident that when my roommates returned to their respective countries, they appreciated that America was not the Great Satan, and shared that message as their circumstances allowed.

Twenty years before me, a young man from Ghana also attended Macalester. He ran on the track team, excelled in oratorical contests, and impressed his professors with his reserved yet resolute demeanor.

Kofi Annan now serves as Secretary General of the United Nations, his work shaped in part by his coming of age in the United States. While he is not afraid to hold America's feet to the fire when he thinks we deserve it,

Annan understands Americans are no different than most of humanity in terms of the values we hold dear.

Finally, let me tell you about another, less celebrated Macalester alumnus. Like me, Tim Haviland graduated from an Iowa high school in 1978. I was from Iowa City and he was from Ames. We took different classes and ran with different crowds, but knew each other well enough to nod politely as we met walking across campus.

Like Kofi Annan, Tim pursued his professional aspirations in New York City. On the morning of September 11, he was developing software in the World Trade Center. He is among the nearly 3,000 souls now dead.

Our public schools have been given many responsibilities beyond the strictly academic. To that list, I add, "Saving the world from mindless hate and violence, one child at a time."

Is that a fair burden for our schools? Of course not. But who ever said life was fair?

Chapter Two

Establishment

UNFUZZY MATH AS A POLITICAL STATEMENT

If I were to tell you our state's dropout rate is 1.75 percent, you'd probably think Iowa is doing a marvelous job of keeping our kids in school through graduation. You'd also probably think anyone arguing otherwise is a misinformed malcontent unwilling to acknowledge mathematical reality.

Well, guess what? Our official dropout rate IS 1.75 percent, but six times that many students don't collect their diplomas. Moreover, you further triple your odds against graduating if you're a member of a minority population. If you think I'm the misinformed malcontent, hang tough with some math, and read on.

According to the Iowa Department of Education (*Condition of Education*, 2001), "A student is considered a dropout if he or she does not complete a district approved K–12 program," and, "The dropout statistic is calculated by dividing the total number of dropouts by the sum of the total enrollment for the corresponding grades."

Given our 1.75 percent dropout rate, is that a fancy way of saying, "There is a 98.25 percent chance Iowa students will graduate from high school"? Until a week ago, I thought the answer was "Yes." Unfortunately, Iowa's DE, like others nationwide, calculates dropouts on a per-year basis, not on a per-student basis. The difference is staggering.

Iowa considers students to be potential dropouts from grades 7–12. Last year, if you divided the number of dropouts by the total 7–12 enrollment, you arrived at a 1.75 percent dropout rate.

Simple enough, right? Not quite. Starting from 7th grade, students don't just need to survive one year of school to graduate, but six. Thus, if you multiply 1.75 percentby six, you get a cumulative "common-sense" dropout rate of 10.5 percent. Quite a difference.

Also remember that kids who drop out one year aren't there the next. If you lost 1.75 percent of 10,000 7th graders, in 8th grade you'd start from 9,825 kids. Each year, like compounding interest in reverse, the base shrinks.

The report doesn't detail dropouts by grade, so it's impossible to determine how many would have made it to graduation, but it does provide average dropout rates, by race and gender, for the past six years—enough to roughly track last year's graduating class.

Do the math, and you find that out of 10,000 theoretical white 7th graders in 1995, 8,977 would have actually graduated in 2001—a real-world dropout rate of 10.23 percent. For African American, Hispanic and American Indian kids, the "common-sense" dropout rates are far worse: 26.22 percent, 30.58 percent, and 30.38 percent, respectively.

Moreover, these rates also only count students enrolled at the start of a school year. If a student leaves AFTER his sophomore year but doesn't return as a junior, he literally "doesn't count." If you compare the 1.75 percent dropout rate, which probably understates dropouts in Grades 9–12, with the average "attrition" rate of 3.17 percent for those years, you'll find that for every two students who officially drop out, a third simply "disappears."

The sound you hear is kids falling through the cracks.

Iowa, alone among the 50 states, requires local school districts to enact and enforce their own academic standards. As a local board member with an academic background in education, I thought a 1.75 percent dropout rate meant a 98.25 percent graduation rate. Seemed reasonable.

If the only way I can understand the real story is to download a massive report from the Internet, plow through 250 pages of tables, and spend several hours crunching spreadsheets, what chance do most members of Iowa's 371 school boards have? Not much.

Who pays the price? The students with whom we've been least successful.

What's particularly disheartening is that our ignorance undermines our ability to make decent decisions. If we think 98 percent of our kids graduate, it's fair to also think we can devote more resources to our top tier because the bottom tier is so small. The dropouts won't quibble, and their parents are unlikely to have the mathematical confidence or political connections to challenge our findings, and resulting fundings, even if they smelled a rat.

Educators tend to be touchy about accountability. We urge you not to obsess over standardized test scores, and implore politicians not to delve too deeply into our business. However, if we ask you to trust us, we must be aggressively honest in return—even when it hurts. Understating our failings by a six-fold measure falls far short of that test. Either we don't understand our data, or it's more convenient for us when you don't. Neither position can be defended.

Fuzzy math became a pejorative term during the 2000 presidential elections, but "unfuzzy math" can be just as disingenuous. Focusing on discrete data that describe only part of a picture is like staring at one bead of a mosaic. There's nothing untrue about what you're seeing, but it's not until you step back from the painting that you really get the picture.

Is Iowa's dropout rate REALLY 1.75 percent? If not, which populations lose when the larger truth lies buried under a pile of partial information? Finally, which groups gain from the mathematical misdirection?

NOW, do you get the picture?

"BETTER BOARDSMANSHIP"? DON'T THINK SO

This column won't win me any points with the Iowa Association of School Boards. In fact, it may cost me a few. The sad part is, the IASB might be keeping track.

The IASB has a program to develop *Better Boardsmanship*. If I earn 75 credits in a year, I get a certificate. If half our board qualifies, we get a plaque. We receive credits for attending workshops such as *Accountability: Road Map to Improvement and Structure: Policies for Improved Governance*, and for "experience and service" activities.

The part of this column that might have the IASB erasing any credits I earned for attending these sessions is that which challenges their claim to having the only opinion worth hearing. You see, each time I "testify on behalf of IASB's official position" before our legislature or state agencies, I get my ticket punched for five credits—and can earn up to 20 credits for parroting the party platform each year.

But should I not toe the IASB line, I get zero credits, even though I can't imagine why my independent testimony would be less valuable to my development as a leader than me mouthing words authorized by the IASB Ministry of Education—unless I've somehow missed the distinction between "education" and "indoctrination."

Of course, neither the IASB nor anyone else has asked me to talk about anything, but that's not the point. What troubles me about the reward system is that it insinuates that knowledge and wisdom do not arise from open and spirited discussions, an odd attitude for a supposed defender of academic values. It also implies diversity is fine in theory, but when it comes to different ideas, "We know what's best for your schools. We prefer you be silent unless spoken to, and then we'll tell you what we want to hear."

That's not just me talking. That's also the considered opinion of John Stuart Mill, whose writings helped shape the U.S. Constitution. In a document the IASB might want to dust off, Mill wrote, "A people, it appears, may be progressive for a certain period of time, and then stop. When does it stop? When it ceases to possess individuality."

One of Mill's intellectual descendants on the U.S. Supreme Court, Felix Frankfurter, put it more plainly when he wrote, "Anybody who is any good is different from anybody else." That hardly sounds like a clarion call for testimony "on behalf of an official position" to me.

Of course, actual diversity is dangerous to established orders. That's why most tend to suck the oxygen from fresh ideas whenever they can, and why it's so inspiring when people have the guts to say what they really think.

My absolute favorite moment during my first year on the school board was when Mark Schneider, the principal of two of our elementary schools, challenged the board to practice what we preach. He pointed out that funding was cut from last year's budget for out-of-state staff development, and then suggested we walk our talk when it came to our conference travel plans.

It's generally not a great career move to imperil your bosses' professional perquisites, but Schneider stood up for what he thought was right—which is exactly as it should be. The alternative is to sulk in silence, an act that—when practiced often enough—turns potential leaders into clock punchers and bureaucrats.

This is more than an argument for intellectual anarchy—it's also the best way I know to rebuild support for our public schools. Why are voters so interested in vouchers, charter schools, home schooling and open enrollment programs? Sure, they want choices, but I think the reason they want choices is that they no longer trust the educational elite when they're told, "We know what's best for your children. Please be silent unless spoken to, and then tell us only what we want to hear."

Most Americans may not know the difference between Felix Frankfurter and an Oscar Mayer wiener, but they do cherish their freedoms—especially to think as they please. Our public school leaders tinker with that liberty at their peril.

One final note. Another way to earn five IASB credits is by writing an article for its newsletter—and you get 10 points if it's published. For the life of me, I can't figure out how a decision to accept an already-written article affects anyone's "boardsmanship," unless, of course, it's another way to get us "on board" with the IASB program.

While I originally wrote these columns for you, my discerning Mid-Prairie readers, I suppose there's no reason I couldn't submit this one to the editors of the *Compass* for publication.

While I always stand ready to be pleasantly surprised, I suspect you're among what will remain a limited audience for these ideas—and that I won't have to clear space on my wall for an IASB *Better Boardsmanship* certificate anytime soon.

NICE WORK IF YOU CAN GET IT

Everyone's heard the not-funny joke about the boy who killed his parents—and then threw himself on the mercy of the court because he was an orphan. Unfortunately, when I hear the old guard of the education industry talk about the looming shortage of teachers, principals and superintendents, it's the first parable that comes to mind.

There's no doubt the numbers are bleak. Forty percent of my state's teachers will qualify for retirement by 2010. This year, 1,600 teachers walked out of our classrooms, never to return. For administrators, who tend to be older, the numbers are even worse.

Colleges of education are finding it hard to recruit collegians blinded by the big bucks of the business world, and many of those they do graduate don't last. In Iowa, 28 percent of our new teachers took off after three or fewer years on the job.

The colleges' solution? More of the same. Sure, they're pushing more money, respect and professional development—all of which are legitimate goals—but the bottom line is that they're talking up the same strategy that put us in this pickle in the first place.

It seems to me that if you're serious about attracting great people to the classroom, you do what every other business does—you focus on talent, attitude and ability, and you help your recruits acquire the skills they need to be successful as soon as possible. You certainly don't limit yourself to kids who identified themselves as teachers-to-be when they were 20-year-old undergraduates, or the even smaller group of adults who can afford to take a multiyear vow of poverty to earn midlife teaching certificates.

That, however, is exactly what we're doing. When I returned to Iowa in 1996, I briefly entertained the notion of becoming a teacher—again. In the 1980s in Alaska, I had completed all but student teaching for an elementary certificate. In the 1990s, I had been tenured as a college professor, earned a doctorate in higher education, and actually had administrative responsibility over a University of Alaska teacher education program.

Still, the University of Iowa told me that to become a teacher in our state, I would need at least two years of undergraduate education classes—a sacrifice I was unable to make. And you wonder why we have a teacher shortage?

Last fall, I attended an Iowa Association of School Boards convention session on the shortage of superintendents. Inside the room were 50 middle-aged men collectively agonizing about the few people in the world who were exactly like them—people who had become teachers in their 20s, principals in their 30s and superintendents in their 40s.

Their solutions? More respect, more money and less work. When I dared to suggest that perhaps we ought to go beyond the people in the room replicating themselves and start trying to attract a few fresh faces— and maybe ideas—to the field, my comments were greeted with responses ranging from polite civility to open derision.

Fortunately, some people are trying to break out of the box in which we have sealed ourselves. At this summer's state Democratic convention, Iowa Governor Tom Vilsack called for "fundamental" changes in the way teachers are compensated, replacing a system tied to longevity with one that rewards classroom results, training and career development.

"I think people in this state will pay for results," said Vilsack. "The public will not mind teachers making more if they are convinced that it will result in better-educated students."

Educators are kidding themselves if they think the only folks who can do their jobs are clones with the correct credentials. Mary Sue Coleman didn't need a degree in higher ed to run the University of Iowa, Bill Gates didn't need an MBA to manage Microsoft, and Bill Cohen wasn't required to have been a foot soldier to lead the U.S. Department of Defense—where the stakes are at least as high as in most school districts.

Education's two modern mantras are diversity and lifelong learning, but the reality is our credentialing processes seem to exclude anyone who has ever done anything else with their professional lives but spend them exclusively in classrooms.

When we dare to step outside our comfort zones, great things can happen. This year, a Wall Street executive was named chancellor of New York City's schools and a former Colorado governor was appointed superintendent in Los Angeles, and both are getting good reviews. More sadly, a former military general serving as Seattle's superintendent was universally mourned when he died too young while successfully turning around that city's schools.

When it comes to creating new educators, we may not be killing our parents—but we are cutting off too much talent from the profession, and our kids will suffer for it. As we work to address our shortages, the education industry might be well-advised to look first at its own practices before seeking redress in the court of public opinion.

OF NO USE TO THE EDUCATIONAL ESTABLISHMENT

Two teacher compensation plans have been introduced in our state legislature. While they differ substantially in the pay raises they promise, they completely diverge when it comes to alternative teacher certification.

Republicans propose that people with bachelor's degrees in fields other than teaching could be granted alternative teaching certificates, provided they take two semester-length summer courses and work during the interim under the direction of a master teacher.

Iowa Governor Vilsack's plan doesn't mention alternative certification at all. That's a nice way of saying, "Forget it."

To lay my cards face up on the table, I am a Republican who voted for Vilsack, a Democrat, and who applauds the obvious passion he has for education. That said, if you discourage otherwise capable people from entering the profession, particularly when we face a devastating teacher shortage in the next decade, you'd better have a darn good reason.

Vilsack's ostensible excuse for doing nothing is to protect teacher quality. I beg to differ, and again, I'll lay my own cards on the table.

I returned to Iowa in 1996 after a 13-year absence (as Vilsack is encouraging other native Iowans to do). Shortly after settling in, I visited the University of Iowa to see what it would take to get Iowa teacher certification. The answer was, "Two years."

Under most circumstances, I think school districts would be interested in talking to someone who grew up "in the neighborhood," studied elementary education with a straight-A average, and had six years' successful teaching experience.

Most districts looking for a government or business faculty member might be interested in someone with degrees in those fields, who's taught economics on three continents, and has served as an elected public official.

Most districts recruiting a journalism teacher might be interested in someone with graduate degrees in journalism and education, who's worked in commercial TV news, and who started a half-hour daily newscast using community college students and an oil company's cast-off camera equipment.

However, because I missed my semester of elementary student teaching to accept a university job offer, I never got certified in Alaska—and unless something changes, I never will in Iowa either.

The day the GOP plan was introduced, a teacher told the *Des Moines Register*, "I don't think a summer course is going to get us where we need to go. We need quality teachers." Well, I'd like to think I was a quality teacher. My university gave me tenure in half the usual time. With "an intense 12-week teacher-training program," a "two-year mentoring and induction program," and another closing course, I suspect I could be brought up to speed.

To be truthful, if alternative certification passed tomorrow, chances are I would not be teaching next fall, eligibility rules aside. I like my job, also in education, and plan to keep it as long as they'll have me.

Had it passed five years ago, though, I might be teaching today — with 30 years between me and retirement. I'd be contributing to our children and to the struggle against our looming teacher shortage — but in my current uncredentialed condition, I'm of no use to the educational establishment.

If universities were serious that to be a good teacher you needed to be certified as such, it would insist upon the same standards for their own faculty (which, of course, would result in campus riots — this time by the "teachers"). Professors get paid to teach subjects they've studied in depth, and work out the pedagogy part by themselves.

It's not a perfect system, but there's no denying America's system of higher education is the world's finest. Unfortunately, many fewer people would make the same claim for our elementary, middle and secondary schools than a generation ago.

At some point, many people who focused on "doing well" early in their careers discover there's more satisfaction in life in "doing good." There are few ways to do more good than to be a teacher, but middle-aged mortgage payers generally aren't able to devote two unpaid years to earning traditional teaching certificates, so they don't — and our children are the poorer for it.

Alternative certification taps into a pool of talent that is currently untouchable. No matter what roads they took to get there, school districts will still hire the best available teaching candidates. I stand ready to be schooled as to why that's a bad thing.

PRESSURE MY MOM

Imagine the headline *MOST HOUSES STILL STANDING!* with no word of the home consumed by flames the previous night. Imagine a newscast showing freely flowing north–south traffic, but ignoring the jackknifed semi jamming the east–west turnpike. Imagine an article praising airlines for their 75 percent on-time arrival rate, but overlooking the 25 percent of flights that arrive late.

John Q. Citizen might revel in the happy news for a while, until he discovered it was his co-worker whose house burned, his spouse who was stuck in traffic, or himself who was stranded at an airport. It's then that he would value candor over contentment.

Numerous surveys rank education as the issue Americans care most about, and that's often reflected in our media coverage and political debate. All that attention should make school supporters happy, but guess again.

In a neighboring community, the school board president recently apologized under pressure for criticizing supposed actions of some staff—and was later scolded in letters to the editor for forgetting the president's job is to be an "unabashed cheerleader" for the district.

Similarly, our state school board association is coaching local board members on how to get positive press. According to the Iowa Association of School Boards, our "facts" should be arranged around five key messages:

1. Our schools are better than ever.
2. Our students are receiving a solid education in the basic skills.
3. Public education is a sound investment and a real value.
4. Our educators are dedicated, caring and qualified.
5. Our schools serve their communities.

The IASB provides statistics to fill out suggested storylines. As proof our schools "are better than ever," it writes "Iowa students consistently score among the nation's best on the ACT college entrance exam, ranking in the top three states nationally for more than a decade. Iowa students scored an average composite of 22.0 on the 36-point exam in 2000, compared with a national average of 21.0."

Demonstrably true, but the "whole truth" is more complicated. According to the Iowa Department of Education, we ranked first on the ACT from 1990–1994, but have since slipped behind Wisconsin and/or Minnesota, which test similar proportions of students. While Iowa's scores have increased 0.2 points in the past 10 years, the national increase was 0.4 points, or twice as much. The percentage of Iowa kids scoring above the national average was 61.8 percent in 1991; in 2000, it was 60.3 percent.

With other tests, the "facts" are even more slippery. For example, 4th graders scoring proficient or higher on the *Iowa Test of Basic Skills* Reading Test fell from 71.4 percent in 1993–1995 to 67.7 percent in 1998–2000, and 8th graders stumbled from 73.5 percent to 69.7 percent. On the *Iowa Tests of Educational Development,* 11th graders scoring proficient or better dropped from 79.1 percent to 75.1 percent. The same backsliding occurred in math.

Our schools are undeniably among the cream of the crop, but I would question anyone who had only good things to say about anything. Pressure my mom, and she'll probably share a story about me. If I know school officials are telling only half the story, as a citizen I become suspicious, and even hope the media assume a more adversarial stance, which hardly advances the cause of positive PR.

Alice Longworth Roosevelt, Theodore's daughter, once said, "If you can't say something good about someone, sit right here by me." We're a long way from that in media coverage of our schools. Photos of kids at science fairs, involved in service learning, or slamming home runs far outnumber stories unfairly slamming our schools. Any other industry would rejoice over the positive coverage we regularly receive.

As educators, we should respect that honest observations, constructive criticism and appropriate praise are all legitimate tools for learning. Most teachers wouldn't accept, "If you can't give a kid an A, don't give him any grade at all," and most coaches couldn't live with, "If you can't yell anything nice about a lay-up, don't yell anything at all."

Part of being in the game is getting your nose bloodied. As a person who wants great schools, I want insightful, balanced and even challenging media coverage—not happy talk. Do that, and spell my name right, and you won't hear any complaints from me.

HERE'S WHAT THE PAPERS WERE ASKING ABOUT

Despite claims to the contrary, no news is *not* good news—it's bad news, and often illegal. That's the conclusion of a recent 14-newspaper investigation into state and local government agency compliance with Iowa's Open Records Law.

As part of their investigation, a purposely low-profile representative of the group wrote a letter to our district asking for a copy of our superintendent's contract, and the results of our composite standardized test scores. Like 80 percent of the other 375 districts around the state, Mid-Prairie did not respond. Our administration does not recall being sent the letter, and the newspapers apparently didn't ask twice. The bottom line is we were published on the newspapers' list of districts found to be out of compliance.

Of all Iowa's government entities, our schools were worst at responding—80 percent of superintendents failed to respond, and 7 percent said the writer would have to examine the records in person. Only 13 percent did what the papers said the Open Records Law required—that is, they sent the contract and the test scores.

This is particularly disconcerting given schools' insistence upon freedom of expression. If school districts expect to be treated with deference in their examination of academic issues, we had better be double-careful about denying others access to the information we control—but may not find convenient or comfortable to share.

According to our sunshine statutes, public records include "all records, documents, tape, or other information, stored or preserved in any medium, or belonging to this state or any county, school corporation . . . whose facilities or indebtedness are supported in whole or in part with property tax revenue."

According to the *Iowa City Gazette,* "Cedar Rapids Superintendent Lew Finch and Marion Superintendent Bill Jacobson were among the many superintendents who did not comply. Finch said he didn't respond because the letter of request raised suspicion with its Des Moines address. Jacobson said recent criticism of school districts' management practices has made superintendents 'a little gun-shy' about such requests."

To state the obvious, it's not Finch's job to question the motives of the letter writer, and Jacobson's reluctance to comply because of "recent criticism of school districts' management practices" is a slam-dunk argument in favor of such disclosures.

While it's too late to take our name off the consortium's list of non-compliers, it's important that our local citizens understand what's going on in our district. This is a broad-brushed summary, but here are our composite scores for reading and math, with "proficiency" defined as scores above the 40th percentile on *Iowa Test of Basic Skills* or *Iowa Tests of Education Development.*

Reading, Grade 4—less than proficient, 37 percent; proficient or advanced, 63 percent. Goal: 70 percent proficient or advanced.

Reading, Grade 8—less than proficient, 22 percent; proficient/advanced, 78 percent. Goal: 70 percent.

Reading, Grade 11—less than proficient, 21 percent; proficient/advanced, 79 percent. Goal: 70 percent.

Math, Grade 4—less than proficient, 31 percent; proficient/advanced, 69 percent. Goal: 72 percent.

Math, Grade 8—less than proficient, 19 percent; proficient/advanced, 81 percent. Goal: 72 percent.

Math, Grade 11—less than proficient, 24 percent; proficient/advanced, 76 percent. Goal: 72 percent.

While I'm a volunteer school board member now, for most of my career I have worked in or taught journalism, so I admittedly have a strong bias in favor of "sunshine" laws—because they serve your right to know. You're paying the bills, and you deserve to know if we're getting the job done.

As the *Gazette* put it, "Don't take this as reporters nosing around in somebody else's business. Those reporters were looking into how you would be treated by public officials. These are your rights, and your rights are being denied. These public officials should not forget you—or your right to public information."

If you want to see the reports of Mid-Prairie's test scores, or the superintendent's contract, feel free to ask our central office for copies, by letter or in person.

As at most Iowa school districts these days, you won't hear "No" for an answer.

I WANT YOU . . . TO BE A TEACHER

The teaching and soldiering professions may not seem to have much in common, but consider this. Both call upon a sense of public service, both need young people to fill their ranks, and both make no promises of careers high in either glamour or salary.

When it comes to recruiting, though, military planners think differently than their civilian counterparts. They advertise. Even the most casual media consumers recognize the slogans *An Army of One* and *The Few, The Proud, The Marines.*

While most advertisers try to persuade you their products will make your life more comfortable, the military doesn't. Remember the slogan, "We do more before 9 o'clock than most people do all day"? As actors in another popular commercial might say, "Nine in the morning? Whassup with that?"

While both education and the armed forces are after the same "demographic," can you recite any marketing pitch aimed at potential teachers, or hum any education jingle? (Alice Cooper's *School's Out* doesn't count). I can't either.

If we're serious about finding more teachers, we have to do what free markets demand. Toward that end, try the following commercials on for size.

MESSAGE ONE: A split screen, with an actor in each half-screen preparing for work. Actor 1 is putting on a suit and tasseled loafers. Actor 2 dons a tie—and tennis shoes.

Both drive to work. Actor 1 is stuck in traffic, with a smoggy skyline in the distance. Actor 2 pulls into a sunny school parking lot, with smiling kids waving at him. Actor 1 waits at a bank of elevators, while Actor 2 recites the *Pledge of Allegiance* with his class.

Actor 1 stares blankly at a computer, then sits at a table with similarly attired peers. Actor 2 works with a student at the chalkboard, then runs the bases in a kickball game.

As the spot ends, Actor 1 looks at the clock, pushes the paper on his desk into his briefcase, and fights the nighttime traffic home. Actor 2 hears the bell ring, packs his things, high-fives several kids as he heads out the door, and drives home—in daylight.

COMMERCIAL TWO: A child sits on her mother's lap, reading a book. Later, she heads to kindergarten, and her mother wipes away a tear. There are quick shots of the girl as she plays in the band, goes to a dance, and receives her diploma. The mother wipes away another tear.

Next, you see the girl in college, then as a student teacher. Later, the girl—now a woman—has a class of her own, and a child shyly places an apple on her desk. Finally, at her retirement, this 65-year-old "girl" is embraced by many of the students whose lives she's touched. This time, *she* wipes away the tear.

COMMERCIAL THREE: Another split-screen. Mother 1 drops off her daughter at a bus stop, while Mother 2 puts her child in her car and heads to school—where she's a teacher. Mother 1 looks at her child's photo on her desk, while Mother 2 greets her daughter in the hallway.

At the end of the day, Child 1 disembarks from the school bus and walks into a day care center. Child 2 enters her mother's classroom, and they walk hand-in-hand to their car. A turning calendar page shows June 21, and you see an entry for Mother 1 that reads "Client Meeting." You then see Mother 2's calendar, which exclaims "Going Fishing!" The spot ends with Mother 2 and her daughter laughing in a canoe.

All three commercials end with the tagline, "It's about more than making money. It's how you SPEND your life." A 1-800 number and a website address follow, through which young adults—and perhaps older adults who recognize themselves in the spots—are directed to an appropriate college of education.

Twenty-year-olds need to be reminded that compensation comes in forms other than paychecks. It's a tough task, but compare that with the military's challenge. They have to persuade kids to want to get sent out on aircraft carriers or stay submerged in submarines for six months at a stretch—and stand a fair chance of being shot at in the bargain.

My guess is the education profession could pull it off. We certainly won't know until we've tried.

WHEN WE STARTED, OR WHEN WE FINISHED?

Less than 24 hours ago, I was walking hand-in-hand with my nine-year-old son when he looked up at me and sweetly asked, "In your day, did people use quill pens instead of pencils?" He was clearly disappointed when I told him the answer was "No."

While I was surprised to learn Patrick thought I predated the pencil, I was perhaps even more perturbed to discover he thought "my day" was done. I may have lost a step, but as basketballers say on the playground, another remark like that and "I'll take you to school."

Of course, when it comes to schools, his "day" is far different than my mine was—and my bet is we both ain't seen nuthin' yet. By the time Patrick earns his high school diploma, there will probably be more changes in education over those eight years than there have been over the past 80—most of them the result of schools scrambling to find solutions as they discover their old answers are no longer up to the task.

We've worked through these upheavals before. Once upon a time, it was standard practice for unmarried women to teach in one-room schools for virtually pennies a day. As schoolhouses consolidated into school buildings and students were slotted into grades, teachers started to demand living wages.

As we enter a new century, it's in a still more money-conscious society that our schools are trying to attract and retain the best possible employees. Toward that end, this spring our school board approved a two-year pay pact with our teachers, a one-year agreement with our support staff, and were scheduled to consider our administrative salaries this week.

In many ways, our contract talks resemble a tug of war, with staff on one end of the rope and the school board on the other. Both sides grab the rope, dig in their heels, and pull as hard as they can. After a lot of grunting, and often bloodied fingers, an accommodation is reached, after which both groups fall exhausted to the ground, hoping to avoid another such ordeal for as long as possible.

Tug of war, by definition, is a zero-sum game in which one side must give ground for the other side to make progress. I would hope in education, success would lie not in recruiting bigger, meaner guys to your side—but in persuading all of us to hitch the rope to whatever it is we want to move (for example, test scores or public opinion), and have everyone pull together to make it happen.

Let's stipulate we all want our students taught by great teachers. If instead of squabbling over nickels in contract negotiations, we were to jointly develop measurable goals for the district, align and fund our staff development to meet those goals, and reward teachers as our goals were reached, we might find more public support for our schools, which might translate into more nickels, and even dollars, for salaries.

It's clear there's less faith than there once was for any American institution that simply says, "Trust us. We'll get the job done." At the same time, there's likely more willingness to reward demonstrated results. What I know for sure is that if we want our teaching staff to benefit from comprehensive professional and public support, and to receive commensurate compensation, we must quit expending so much energy tugging on opposite ends of our rope and start pulling as a team.

Now that we have two years to develop a new pay package, we have an unparalleled opportunity to find common ground. While we may never be able to offer Washington, D.C., salaries at Washington Township Elementary School, we can offer the chance to work where schools are safe, commutes are short, real estate is reasonable, and where teachers can make fundamental contributions to their communities. If our staff can do all that, and still make a decent living, that should be worth something.

Ever since one-room schoolhouses—and quill pens—went out of style, education has been dominated by a one-size-fits-all mentality. That model worked for decades, but "its day" is rapidly coming to an end. Thirty years from now, when Patrick's child looks him in the eye and asks, "Dad, what was school like in your day?" he may have to ask in return, "You mean when I started, or when I finished?"

Like it or not, my guess is that the answers will be far different.

EVERYONE ON THE SAME PAIGE

I caught a lucky break last week. Sledding on a sunny Saturday with my kids, I twice caught air during an exciting downhill run, slamming the ground hard after each freefall. After a couple hours' denial, I hobbled to the hospital, discovering I had fractured a vertebra about two-thirds of the way down my spine.

I call it a "lucky break" because I had no tingling, numbness or paralysis, which are far worse misfortunes than any short-term discomfort. While I'll have to spend the next six weeks in a back brace, by springtime the spring should be back in my step—something for which I'll be forever grateful.

And—from an educational perspective—spending five days as a hospital guest gave me lots of time to watch George W. Bush's cabinet confirmation hearings on TV, including those of Rod Paige, the Houston superintendent tabbed to be the next U.S. Secretary of Education.

The hearings were a love-in for Paige, who two months ago was named Superintendent of the Year by the National Alliance of Black Educators. Although he supports the limited use of educational vouchers, progressive Democratic Congresswoman Sheila Jackson Lee introduced Paige as "a man committed to excellence, an educator who believes every child can learn and every child can succeed."

While Paige complained Jackson Lee "laid it on thick," he was clearly comfortable in repeating the refrain that brought him to the head of the class. Paige told the senators, "Some don't want us to set clear goals in the classroom and others don't want us to demand that schools get the job done. If we had listened to such advice in my own school district years ago, we would never have seen the improvements in student achievement that we have experienced."

From a local perspective, the most pointed questions came from (the late) Minnesota Senator Paul Wellstone. A former college professor who struggled in school and with tests because of a learning disability, Wellstone pressed Paige on standardized testing and accountability, two frequent topics of "conversation" in our district this year.

Wellstone asked if Paige could promise the committee he would never rely on a single test to determine whether students advance from one grade to another, or if teachers get raises—and to pledge that federal funds would never be contingent upon the outcomes of these single measures.

Paige agreed multiple measures were much preferred, and then put the question in a different light. He said too many people think tests are used to punish students and schools. Paige said he wanted to know if kids were learning and, if they weren't, he wanted to have the data necessary to ensure effective changes got made fast.

When it came to accountability, Paige argued standards weren't meant to punish poor performers, but to promote excellence. In the nicest possible way, he said "as a matter of principle" that any entity providing funds has the right to expect evidence the money is doing good—and that would include the federal government.

Wellstone agreed—an unexpected outcome that made him laugh out loud, and almost had me falling out my hospital bed in shock. Senator Edward M. Kennedy called his committee's overwhelming support of Paige "an auspicious signal that we can work well together on education in the new Congress," and expressed his hope that "the issue of education will set the standard for bipartisan cooperation over the next four years."

With Jackson Lee, Wellstone, Kennedy and Paige all singing from the same songsheet, it may be this year will mark a break with the more confrontational ways we've often discussed our common commitment to education.

And although I'm still not complaining, I also hope it's the last major "break" I encounter for a long while.

Chapter Three

Curriculum

LESSONS FROM OUR "POOREST" STUDENTS

If you're like me, you have some ideas as to why poor kids do poorly in school. Their parents didn't go far in school, so the kids don't have good role models. Their parents may not work regularly, so they don't see the discipline it takes to hold a job. They're poor, so they don't have books around the house.

And finally, although it's not nice to mention in polite company, their parents may have set low standards for themselves, and they may have the same low aspirations for their children.

The trouble with all these reasons is that they're demonstrably wrong.

So, if it isn't the families' fault, then whose fault is it? If you ask the poor kids, their answers are almost insulting: "School is boring," "My classes are irrelevant" and "No one ever challenges me." While not as nuanced as our answers, it turns out—based upon studies examined by the Education Trust—it's the kids who are right.

You're probably thinking, "Yeah, right. If school is so easy, then why are they failing?" The answer is schools channel children they expect to do poorly into the least challenging classes taught by the least effective teachers. Over time, these students grow disinterested in learning, and ultimately academically disabled. Our schools—which crippled these kids in the first place—then turn around with ready-made excuses: "It's not us. We tried to make it easy. It's their families—and that's society's problem, not ours."

The evidence bears out this harsh reality.

A Harvard study of Texas schools found that teacher quality—measured by education, experience and test scores—had far more impact on student success than any other factor, including family income and parent education.

A University of Tennessee study found that students who scored the same on mathematics tests in 3rd grade were separated by as much as 50 percentile points by 6th grade, depending solely upon the quality of the teachers to whom they were assigned.

In Boston, researchers found that the scores of students with the most effective math teachers went up an average of 15 percentile points in one year, while those with the least effective teachers actually went down a point.

If you accept that teacher quality makes a huge difference in student achievement, then if certain students consistently get the worst teachers, the reason these kids fail may not result from what they brought to the classroom, but from what the classroom brought to them.

Speaking to the Iowa Association of School Boards last fall, Kati Haycock of the Education Trust reported that even poor and minority children who score *higher* on standardized tests than wealthier, whiter kids are more likely to be diverted from the honors track and toward remedial classrooms. The best teachers tend to teach the highest-level courses, so the poor kids end up with the worst instructors and the least challenging curriculum. Hence, they're bored by irrelevant, unchallenging classes—just as they reported.

"The research could not be more clear, consistent or compelling," says Haycock. "It supports what parents have known all along: teacher quality matters a lot. Effective teachers can help students achieve enormous gains, while ineffective teachers can do great and lasting damage."

To remedy the problem, the Education Trust recommends all school districts have clear instructional and assessment standards, teach more reading and mathematics, help struggling students before they fall behind, involve parents, and implement accountability systems with real consequences for adults in the school.

What does that mean for our district? While we do not experience the impoverishment of many school districts, we have our share of disadvantaged children—and we need to be doubly sure every poor or minority child in our classrooms is challenged to succeed, and not protected from harder classes out of ill-founded concern for their self-esteem.

It means making sure that no student—poor or wealthy, black or white—ever gets saddled with a substandard teacher. If a teacher isn't measuring up, we need to help him or her become proficient, or find a new line of work. The cost of continued failure is just too high.

We also need to figure out a way to reward instructional excellence. Few other jobs pay people basically the same amount no matter the quality of work they perform. While it's not board policy, I wish I could let every teacher in the district know that if they put out for their students, we'll put out for them.

Other districts, with far more entrenched and serious problems than we might have, have turned the corner, and we should learn from their successes. According to Haycock, "These schools—the students, teachers and administrators—are all myth-busters. They show that it can be done. And they show how it can be done.

"What these schools are doing works. And it's not magic, nor are the policies unique to any special teachers or principals. These are common-sense and replicable policies and practices that work. Others interested in boosting student achievement should take notice."

THE NIGHTMARE

Nearly every mathematics student has had *The Nightmare*. In this dream, you show up for a final test in a math class you've never attended, that covers concepts you do not comprehend, and which you are certain to fail. You are utterly alone and helpless. Although you eventually wake up and realize "it was all a dream," you retain a nagging fear this nightmare could come true at any time.

I hadn't experienced *The Nightmare* for 20 years—until several Mid-Prairie mathematicians appeared before the school board, toting questions they recently tackled in a Math League contest. If you're prone to bad dreams, you may want to skip the next sentence, which contains the "easiest" question of the bunch. (For those still with me: "In what base is the number 2001 equal to the base 10 number 55?")

As in *The Nightmare,* not only did I not know the answer, I didn't even understand the question. However, according to Robert Moses, author of *Radical Equations: Math Literacy and Civil Rights,* being

able to battle brain-benders like these may be the ticket to full participation in American life.

"I believe the absence of math literacy in urban and rural communities
throughout this country is an issue as urgent as the lack of registered black
voters in Mississippi was in 1961," says Moses. "And I believe that solv-
ing the problem requires exactly the same kind of community organizing
that changed the South in the 1960s."

Moses knows what he's talking about. He worked side by side with
Martin Luther King 40 years ago. Now, with support from the National
Science Foundation and his MacArthur Foundation "Genius Grant,"
Moses heads a program that teaches 40,000 kids a year abstract mathe-
matics, starting in the 6th grade.

His radical approach to teaching math includes teaching it "back-
wards." Instead of starting with the equations that fill most textbooks, he
uses physical items first (for example, gumdrops to illustrate exponential
growth). He moves on to pictures, then his students' own words, then
proper English, and finally ends with equations.

Lee Stiff, president of the National Council of Teachers of Mathematics,
wouldn't comment on Moses's pedagogical principles to *USA Today*, but
did concede "any program that tries to help kids appreciate why algebra is
important to them in their lives, and why they are being taught the concept,
is a good thing."

The importance of Moses's work extends beyond mere math. Reviewer
Rich Gibson writes that Moses grasps "the unity of ideas and social practice in a classroom where the goal is to struggle for what is true. Robert
Moses's main message is, I think, 'What you do counts.' Makes double
good sense in a math classroom."

Our math contestants left the board speechless, but will have big voices
in our nation's future. Over the next few years, they will take advanced
placement tests in high school, still harder courses in college, and eventually will advance our understanding of the world through their ability to
describe it with numbers. That kind of power can literally change the
world, whether it's Mississippi in 1961 or Mid-Prairie in 2001.

Oh, yeah—2001. Back to the question that started this column: "In
what base is the number 2001 equal to the base 10 number 55?"

The answer is "3." To explain, in base 10, 55 equals 5 tens (5 × 10 to
the first power) plus 5 ones (5 × 10 to the zero power).

In base 3, 2001 equals 2 times three to the third power (or 2 × 27), 0 × three to the second power (or 0 × 9), 0 × three to the first power (or 0 × 3), plus 1 times three to the zero power (or 1 × 1). In other words, 54 + 0 + 0 + 1 = 55.

I apologize for any nightmares that may result from my interpretation of the answer provided to our board out of pity (which I STILL barely understand), but we should all sleep easier knowing our students independently came up with the answer to it and nine even tougher questions.

Civil rights pioneer Robert Moses believes education, and especially mathematics, is society's most effective "leveling" institution. I may not be a certified genius like he is, but I know it leveled me.

KINDERGARTEN ROUNDS UP

For the 17 months I've been on the school board, I've heard plenty about the merits of all-day everyday kindergarten, and was as pleased as most when the board approved the program for next year—but not as pleased as some. The reason? I haven't put in the time they have.

For many veterans, the struggle lasted not 17 months, but 17 years or even longer. What made its advocates persevere over a generation of youngsters? As we establish next year's program, a brief historical review might help us understand the reasons.

In 1965, when I started school, 15 percent of America's kids didn't go to kindergarten at all. Most of my "cohort" attended half-day programs like mine, tromping home at noon. As late as 1972, fewer than 10 percent of 5-year-olds stayed in school all day long.

However, I was among the last of the dinosaurs. By 1980, 96 percent of such kids were in kindergarten, and by 1985, 58 percent were in full-day programs. Do the math and you'll discover the hours spent in kindergarten jumped 65 percent in one generation, from 3.2 to 5.3 hours per day.

Many of these students were also alumni of programs nearly nonexistent in my time, such as nursery school, day care and Head Start. According to a study from that era, "These children are ready for a richer and more diversified program. . . . The evidence clearly indicates that many young children, particularly the urban poor, will experience greater success in school if they are provided a well-planned, all-day kindergarten program."

Not only were the children changing, so were their families. In 1965, I came home at noon to Mom, as did virtually all my friends. A generation later, both Mom and Dad were likely to be working outside the home. As a result, full-day kindergartens not only meant more time learning for the kids, but more time earning for the family.

Surveys conducted as part of our current superintendent search confirm what most of us know; we are home to a generally conservative population. Still, a study conducted three years ago also found we supported all-day everyday kindergarten over part-time programs by a better than 2-to-1 margin (66 percent to 28 percent, respectively).

With the educational and survey data firmly supporting all-day everyday classes, money was the final sticking point. That argument imploded when the state provided our district an unexpectedly large amount we could apply to our program next year.

Not only will the money pay for teachers, it will also staunch the hemorrhaging of students "enrolling out" of our district, choosing instead to enroll in nearby districts offering this program. (Select any district you like; we're the last among the 28 in our region to offer the all-day everyday option.)

For each student who enrolls out, we lose $4,500 in state funds each year. History tells us if we lose kids their first year, we usually lose them their entire academic careers. Multiply $4,500 times 13 years, and you're talking $58,500 in constant dollars per child. In the words of a 1983 study examining this exact same issue in Indiana (with far fewer dollars involved), "School systems simply cannot afford not to implement a full-day schedule." It's too bad we took nearly 20 years to come to the same conclusion.

In approving all-day everyday kindergarten, the board made certain that for parents who believe an alternate-day schedule is best for their children, that option will remain available. Starting next year, parents will be able to choose what's right for their kids, rather than have no choice at all—unless you count leaving the district as a legitimate alternative, which I hope none of us ever will.

In short, the advent of all-day everyday kindergarten represents a time to celebrate—for teachers, taxpayers, and especially children. Like money compounding in a savings account, education prospers when investments are made as early and as often as possible.

I wish I had socked more away in my account when I was 5. Nonetheless, I'm happy to report our next generation of students, and our community as a whole, will someday be far richer for our enlightened investment in their future.

IF WE HAVE CLOSED ANY DOORS, WE HAVE FAILED

Strip away everything else about education—curriculum, teachers, buses, budgets—and in my mind, two words define the enterprise: *options* and *decisions.*

Options are what our schools should make available to our children. If our students graduate from Mid-Prairie able to realistically contemplate becoming a farmer, physician, preacher or president, we've done our job. If we have closed any of those doors, we have failed.

Decisions are what our schools should help give our children the wisdom to make. If we have succeeded only in stuffing our kids' heads with facts, and not helped them learn to sift the useful from the foolish, again we have fallen short.

A growing number of parents believe that while schools might be good at providing options, they're not well-equipped to impart wisdom—and have taken matters into their own hands. More than 1.3 million Americans are home-schooled, and our district has the highest proportion of home-schooled children in Iowa.

Not only is Mid-Prairie's Home School Assistance Program more popular than any other, it's also unique in its character. Instead of using our teachers to directly provide instruction, our district only links home-schoolers and contracted teachers. Unlike our peer districts, ours has no control over the curriculum. To ensure we were doing what we could—and should—to be of assistance within the boundaries the home-school population had set for us, this fall the board asked the contracted teachers to conduct a satisfaction survey.

Nearly three-fourths of the families responded. There was unanimous approval regarding the program's support for each family's philosophy of learning, respect for individual choices and usefulness of group activities. More than three-quarters gave the program the highest possible grade, and all would "recommend this program to a friend."

Clearly, the parents are pleased, but does home-schooling work? A study conducted by the *ERIC Clearinghouse on Assessment and Evaluation* found the average home-schooled children in the 4th and 8th grades scored at the 80th percentile on nationally standardized tests. The U.S. average, of course, is the 50th.

Why do they do so well? One reason is home-schoolers watch less than an hour of TV per day, compared with the national average of three hours. Another is their parents tend to have more formal education, higher incomes, and a much higher chance of being certified teachers themselves.

At the board meeting where these findings were discussed, the teachers were asked how home-schoolers maintained motivation in the absence of "peer pressure to succeed." Admittedly, I'm a graduate of a different district, but let's just say in my day, the "brains" tended not to get the girls. Compare that environment with one where parents are involved in every aspect of their children's education, and make daily sacrifices to ensure their kids are learning, and you can see why home-schoolers do so well.

Are home-schooling and in-class instruction incompatible? I don't think so. As a board member, it's my job to ensure our resources help every student in our district, whether they choose to study in classrooms or around the kitchen table. It's also my opinion that many of our traditionally schooled students could learn from the examples set by families who have taken direct responsibility for their kids' educations.

While I would be hard-pressed to teach Chaucer, calculus or chemistry, my children might benefit from seeing me try. To be honest, I've probably forgotten most of the "things" I learned in high school anyway. What I have remembered is how to conduct research, think through problems and get my work done. There's nothing in home school incompatible with any of those skills.

We live in a community where many people have chosen to lead lives different from the larger society. You can see that in the buggies that travel down our roads, and in smaller acts of rebellion—which includes my own family's disconnection of our TV antenna and prohibition of video games.

Warren Christopher is no recluse, but this week, our nation's former chief diplomat wrote an article in *USA Today* in which he encouraged our students to truly think about what they're learning in school.

"Education is about more than acquiring the information necessary to make money. School is preparation for life, and life involves a great deal more than one's checking account. There is no inevitable correlation between wealth and such attributes as wisdom and judgment. Yet without those qualities, life—no matter how posh or privileged—is going to be difficult and incomplete.

"A broad education—one that explores ideas that are fundamental to human endeavor or that illuminate the human condition—puts our values, accomplishments and accumulations into perspective. Such an education is the bedrock of good judgment and, perhaps more important, of humility."

Christopher described himself in his byline as "a father, grandfather and former U.S. Secretary of State." He sounds like a man more concerned about what his grandchildren are learning than the schools they are attending.

The same should be true for all of us.

SCHOOL TO WORK—AND WORK TO SCHOOL

Ask kindergartners what they want to be when they grow up, and they'll have answers. A dancer! A doctor! A football player! Ask 5th graders, and the replies start getting fuzzy. Ask a high school senior, and your response might be a shrug—and silence.

To help all our students, from kindergarten through 12th grade, have enthusiastic, informed answers to "What do you want to do when you grow up?" in December the Mid-Prairie School District submitted a $65,000 School-to-Work grant application to the Iowa Department of Education, which administers the funds on behalf of the federal government. After passing the first cut, local business leaders and school district representatives met with visitors from the state to make our case. The onsite evaluation went well, and the congratulatory phone call came one day later.

The essence of the School-to-Work initiative is encapsulated in its third goal, "Develop continuity between school-based and work-based learning." With the help of the new funding, our youngest students will participate in Career Awareness Days and Adopt-A-Business programs. By 6th grade, they will develop Personalized Education Plans linking their classroom activities to the skills they will need to succeed at work. Before they graduate, they'll participate in job-shadowing programs, internships, and service learning projects.

The grant will enable Mid-Prairie to hire a half-time coordinator to recruit new business partnerships for the district, as well as integrate
School-to-Work activities across the curriculum. Now, instead of having
career-oriented activities come and go with the ebb and flow of teachers,
there will be an all-building, across-the-district effort to capitalize on the
best ideas available anywhere.

The need for good ideas is overwhelming. As noted in Principal Gerry
Beeler's grant application, more than 75 percent of high school students
nationally plan on earning four-year college degrees, but only 25 percent
get their college diplomas. For Mid-Prairie students, 70 percent plan to attend a two- or four-year college, but only 20 percent challenge themselves
in high school with Advanced Placement or articulated college courses.

While postsecondary education is a prerequisite for most good jobs in
our modern economy, it's not just for those aspiring to white-collar careers. As was noted during a grant orientation session, if you plan to lay
carpet for a living, you not only need to know how to handle a hammer,
you had better be able to calculate square footage and determine angles.
Once you figure that out, your algebra and geometry classes suddenly become a lot more interesting.

Furthermore, if you plan to make a career in carpeting, you also had better
know a few other ABC's—for example, accounting, biology and chemistry.
You're not going to be successful if you can't keep your accounts balanced.
Your customers won't be happy if their carpets' biological systems are dominated by fungi and fleas. And if you want to keep up with your competition,
you better know about polymers like rayon and nylon, not to mention the
chemistry required to keep tiny flora and fauna at bay.

How do you make those connections? With experience, that is exactly
what "School-to-Work" supplies. With this grant, not only will our students understand how their educational efforts "pay off" in the real world,
they will also become ambassadors for our educational community. Instead of being secluded high atop a hill in Wellman, for a few hours each
week our kids will be at the next workstation—whether it's a computer,
an assembly machine or a mechanic's bay.

Leaving the classroom to enhance education seems counterintuitive, but
the truth is learning works best when you can clearly calculate the effort-to-
reward ratio. There's also one other truth today's students had better get used
to—the road between the classroom and the workplace runs both ways.

The days of going to school, graduating, and never needing to know anything else are long gone. It may be called *School-to-Work* as a 17-year-old, but it will be *Work-to-School* the rest of their lives. For our students, Mid-Prairie's successful $65,000 grant application represents an outstanding opportunity to get started on lifelong journeys of academic and professional achievement.

HATS OFF TO OUR CISCO KIDS

In 1907, the *Cisco Kid* arrived in America. Introduced in a short story by O. Henry, the romantic caballero stole the hearts of countless senoritas with his swashbuckling heroism.

Nearly a century later, a new Cisco Kid—the "Cisco Academy"—is just about to ride into Mid-Prairie High School. Despite my status as a reasonably mature adult, I'm not afraid to say I'm smitten by this new development.

The Cisco Academy will allow Mid-Prairie students to leverage the resources of Cisco Systems, the world's most successful Internet services corporation; Kirkwood Community College, perhaps America's most respected community college; and McLeod USA, one of the nation's fastest-growing telecommunications providers.

If all the parties follow up on their commitments, which we expect, the academy will allow Mid-Prairie students to get state-of-the-art training in a trailblazing technology. Should our students successfully complete the online program, which is facilitated by onsite Mid-Prairie faculty, they will earn official recognition as "Certified Computer Network Associates."

As a CCNA, a Golden Hawk would literally have a world of opportunity before him or her. Should they choose to directly enter the workplace after high school, CCNAs will have options far more lucrative than those typically available to 18-year-olds, including many close to home. Moreover, McLeod has all but promised positions to those successfully completing the Cisco curriculum.

On the other hand, should our young CCNAs decide to pursue more education, they could have a semester's worth of Cisco-related credit hours on their transcripts as they enroll in college, plus any they might receive from Mid-Prairie's advanced placement courses. It's entirely realistic to imagine an M-P graduate "entering" college as a sophomore—which means a year's head start on a diploma, and a year's less tuition for Mom and Dad.

The Cisco Academy is perhaps the single most exciting development at the secondary level I've seen during my time on our board. Much of the credit goes to principal Gerry Beeler and teacher Jim Cayton. They followed up on Cisco's overtures, and committed to the training and teaching time required for Mr. Cayton to deliver the curriculum.

What's especially exhilarating about the Academy is that in addition to providing our students with highly sought-after credentials, it teaches our district how to work online to enhance our curriculum. It also provides us with a model for developing cooperative ventures with businesses and postsecondary institutions, a skill our district must develop if it is to thrive in the next generation.

With 1,250 students, Mid-Prairie cannot offer a curriculum spanning all possible academic endeavors. However, if we can appropriately exploit "e"-ducation with the assistance of the right instructional partners, our possibilities are virtually limitless. The implementation of the Mid-Prairie Cisco Academy is a huge step toward that vision.

Duncan Renaldo, the most prolific of the *Cisco Kid* actors, once told an interviewer, "We are now such a nation of hysterical people, running around, with no direction. When I played Cisco, I wanted the world to see a different face, a man of generosity. . . . Cisco was a friend to a better world."

As we implement our Cisco Academy, we should tip our collective hats to Mr. Renaldo, who succeeded in making the original Cisco an American icon, and to Mr. Beeler and to Mr. Cayton, who are successfully partnering with the modern Cisco to make Mid-Prairie an even better school district.

Hats off to all for jobs well done.

CHANNEL ONE FOR ALL, AND ALL FOR *CHANNEL ONE*?

Suppose you had a companion with whom you spent several hours each day. Sometimes funny or profound, but more often witless and profane, this "friend" delighted in pointing out your many deficiencies—all of which he offered to fix, for a price.

How long would it take to kick this creep out of your life? Two minutes? In a million years, would you ask him to take his act to your kids' school? Not likely—but the reality is that in 12,000 American high schools, some say we already have.

This "friend," of course, is television, and the medium's most prominent caller in our classrooms is *Channel One*. This program broadcasts 10 minutes of news and 2 minutes of advertising to 8.1 million kids each school day, reaching five times as many teenagers as the daily news shows of ABC, CBS, NBC and CNN combined. In exchange for its daily 12 minutes, *Channel One* gives each school thousands of dollars worth of media equipment, and free access to a library of first-class educational videos.

Although free, Iowa City's schools are reconsidering whether *Channel One* is worth the cost. Some board members believe the time spent watching the show—12 minutes a day—comes at too high a price, especially if its implicit goal is to turn our kids into junk-food feasting proto-consumers.

Because of my peculiar background, I've paid particular attention to this debate. I started my career as a television reporter before joining the University of Alaska to teach journalism and public relations.

Like the fellow who makes sausage for a living, I know too well the quality of the ingredients going into most TV. Shortly after I left the business in 1996, our family pulled the plug on all the TV antennas going into our house. The garbage-to-good stuff ratio was just too high.

With that background, I was leery of *Channel One* at first—but unlike some Iowa City board members, I've concluded the program can be as legitimate a tool for educating our children as most lectures.

This school year, *Channel One* has aired the following stories—*Teen Views: AIDS in Africa; Youth Violence: Whose Fault Is It?*; and *Should You Pray Before You Play?* Each of these stories has the potential to enliven academic discussions and expose kids to the world beyond their classroom walls.

You probably wouldn't imagine most clergy are major media fans, but even the Jesuit Communication Project contends that ignoring the impact of mass media on our society makes about as much sense as ignoring the effect of biology on the environment.

"The media have a lot to teach us, especially in our schools," writes Father John Pungente. "The three traditional agents of education—home, school, Church—have now been joined by another agent, the mass media.

"As we come to understand the central position that media occupies in the cultural, religious, social and political life of our world, it is not surprising that we want to study it. What is surprising is that it has taken us so long to come to this point."

I applaud what the Iowa City board members are doing—thinking critically about the role of media in our schools. We should always be doing the same, not only with *Channel One*, but with all aspects of our curriculum.

Information has the power to enlighten, enrage and inspire. If we allow our students to do nothing more than sit slack-jawed before glowing tubes, *Channel One* is a waste, and we shouldn't hesitate to show the freeloader the door.

On the other hand, if we help our students actively explore what they're watching, and therefore better understand the world in which they live, we should welcome the service to our schools as we might one of our most well-traveled, articulate and fascinating friends.

ON THE ROAD TO REGIONAL ACADEMIES

Ten years ago this summer, I drove down Alaska's Richardson Highway from Fairbanks to Valdez to build a broadcast journalism program designed to serve the state's native population. Valdez, with a population of 4,000 and the nearest larger town more than 250 road miles away, was thought to be a haven where kids from the even more rural "bush" could learn to start their own community radio and television stations.

It was great idea, but in terms of numbers, a dismal failure. While its handful of students received excellent experience—we started up the region's sole TV station using only classroom talent—we never reached the critical mass of students required to make the program fiscally sustainable.

Many of Iowa's rural school districts suffer from the same problem—there simply aren't enough students to support specialized academic offerings. Districts are forced to choose between paying exorbitant per-pupil rates to subsidize low-enrollment classes or discontinuing the classes altogether, thereby cutting adrift students who would benefit from capstone courses in progressive disciplines such as math and science.

With some courage, Ted Stilwill, director of the Iowa Department of Education, has stepped into this minefield. Speaking recently on *Iowa Press*, Stilwill suggested creating "regional academies" to ensure students have access to advanced courses.

"I think the part of the educational system that is least efficient right now and is costing us the most, that we can change, is our high school programs, and particularly the last two years of high school," said Stilwill. "We can think about creating regional academies that can serve the needs of kids in rural areas, and frankly urban areas, by consolidating those kids who need advanced programs."

Stilwill describes the schools most challenged by their size as those with 200 or fewer students, of which there are 125 in Iowa. Does that mean shutting down high schools just smaller than Mid-Prairie, which has 332 students? More to the point locally, even if we make the cut, what does Stilwill's solution mean for our students?

Let's start with some simple math. Any money a district overspends on low-enrollment courses means we must underspend on classes with more students. Since we work with one budget, not only does that affect learning at the high school level, but all the way down to our kindergarten classrooms.

Does that mean we should start "dumbing down" our high school curriculum, thereby discouraging our highest achieving students? No. What it does mean is figuring out new ways to skin the cat, creating challenging opportunities for students while at the same time spending our limited dollars wisely.

In addition to Stilwill's academies, we have entities that could help—most notably, community colleges. At my college in Alaska, students came to us for courses Valdez High School couldn't offer, and we had instructors teaching advanced placement courses at the high school itself. This allowed both institutions to teach to their advantage, and students to rack up college credits before leaving high school—including some who never thought of themselves as "college material."

Of course, that was in the dark ages of cyberspace. These days, geography is no longer destiny. With the Internet making the marginal cost of video and audio transmissions basically free, there's little reason students sitting in central Iowa couldn't participate in a Mandarin Chinese class originating in South Central Los Angeles, or that a kid in Connecticut couldn't learn from our great program in agricultural education.

Today's students and parents have options. Whether they select home-schooling or enrolling in a larger nearby district, we'll start to lose a few of our best students around the edges, further eroding the head counts in our already hardest-to-fill classes.

What about the teachers for these classes? In my case, I decided I didn't want to spend my limited time on this planet teaching only a handful of kids. As far as I was concerned, I was leaving too few footprints—probably reaching that conclusion only shortly before the University of Alaska would have on its own.

So, when the occasion presented itself, I started teaching introductory computer classes, although I had to teach myself how to use spreadsheets and databases first. Within a year, I went from our "least productive" faculty member to generating more credit hours than any other—and we still got our TV station started on the side.

If we expect our students to learn new skills and take on new knowledge, we should expect no less of our ourselves. This is the most exciting time in the history of education. I hope we have the wisdom to seize upon the world of opportunity before us.

FROM QUADRICYLES TO TERRASERVER.COM

Imagine life in 1901. Henry Ford was building "quadricycles," Orville and Wilbur Wright were earthbound bicycle mechanics, and students stood at blackboards learning to read, write and do arithmetic.

Now, look at 2001. Our automobiles have quadraphonic sound, we fly farther in an hour than the Wright brothers flew in their lifetimes—and students stand at blackboards learning to read, write and do arithmetic.

Some proponents of educational technology claim students could learn at a 21st-century pace if they were provided the same tools today's "knowledge workers" take for granted. Skeptics, on the other hand, see children adding and subtracting on calculators and despair for our future.

The truth, I suspect, lies in between. If I had to write this column "longhand," an archaic term my kids don't even recognize, I wouldn't have the time or energy to do it. At the same time, it's hard to believe that a student's reference skills are much enhanced by typing "Teddy Roosevelt," our president in 1901, into the Google search engine and having it churn out 60,700 website "hits" in 0.08 seconds (my actual results).

If you're a teacher and want to develop your students' fact-finding skills, do you hush up this near-miraculous reference tool so kids learn to crack open actual books—or do you happily introduce them to state-of-the-art library science?

Again, the answer might be in the middle.

Case in point—www.terraserver.com. I recently read that this site, which features U.S. Geological Survey satellite photographs of every inch of American soil, was film critic Roger Ebert's favorite. I figured if Ebert gave it a "Thumbs Up," it must be good. I wasn't disappointed.

Upon arriving at terraserver.com, I saw a world map, and clicked on a spot that approximated Iowa. That brought me to the United States. Another click got me to the Midwest, and a fourth click put me four miles north of Riverside.

By clicking along Highway 22, I soon came to my home, Kalona. Zooming in, I identified Kalona Elementary School, and two blocks west and one block north, picked out my house—as seen from space May 20, 1994. With a one-meter resolution, had someone been tanning on our driveway, I might have seen that too.

I don't know about you, but I think that's really cool (and spooky)—and I bet most kids would agree. Imagine the assignment, "Find your house from outer space, using an atlas and the Internet, and print the picture."

Like me, students would zero in on their homes or farms. Instead of hitting Riverside, they might land in Amana or Cotter, as I did on my second and third tries. Unless they really knew their geography, that would force them into their atlases, where they could see how their targets related to where they actually "landed."

They would have to "click" north, south, east or west as required, ingraining those concepts into their young minds. They would also have to determine which scale makes the most sense for finding a city (a big one), and which helps you find your farm (as small as possible), which would help them make more sense of paper maps next time around.

While there are just a few local residents who were around in 1901, another benefit would be the ability of our youngsters to share their photos with people for whom space travel is a relatively recent phenomenon. Just as our senior citizens might get a kick from seeing the old homestead from outer space, our kids would benefit even more from learning about life before electrification, indoor plumbing, calculators or computers.

As we develop our budget priorities, it's important to remember that technology is just a tool. Just as writing with a sharp pencil probably didn't transform you into your generation's Shakespeare, buying your daughter a Pentium 4 may not morph her into a modern-day Einstein.

However, if a tool helps a student better understand our world, we shouldn't shy from appropriate investments in technology.

Until two weeks ago, I thought I knew what my town looked like, but I had never seen it from space. Now that I have, I'll never look at it quite the same way again. We should make sure all our students have the same opportunities.

DON'T JUDGE AN eBOOK BY ITS COVER

I went to Barnes and Noble today and picked up a few books—20, to be exact. My selections ranged from *Huckleberry Finn* to *Frankenstein,* and from *The Scarlet Letter* to *The Secret Garden*.

You'd think I'd be sore, lugging home 40 or 50 pounds of literature, but although it's 90 degrees outside, I didn't break a sweat.

You might also think I'd be broke. Twenty books at 20 bucks a pop makes for a $400 tab, but I didn't even dent my wallet.

How did I pull off this physical and fiscal feat? Well, I did have to lift a finger, but just one—the one that clicks the mouse on my computer.

Barnesandnoble.com is inviting the world to pick up free copies of 100 different "eBooks." With the right (also free) software, eBooks can be read on most personal computers, as well as on several models of book-sized readers.

B & N is apparently hoping that while we're browsing the bargain bin, we might find a few of its conventionally priced offerings worthy of consideration. I also suspect they're hoping we like the e-reading experience so much that we eventually choose to plunk down a couple hundred dollars for one of their backlit, back-packable electronic readers.

What does this have to do with the our local schools? Read on (the old-fashioned way, on paper).

Each year, Mid-Prairie buys tons of textbooks (no exaggeration). While the numbers vary depending upon our curricular needs and bank balance, we'd "like" to spend about $70,000 annually. While that sounds like a lot, with some textbooks running $70 a copy, that can mean fewer than one new book per student per year.

That also means the typical textbook is replaced about once each decade. By the time its days are done, the book has probably been dunked in a few puddles, marked up by a slew of well-meaning students, and chewed on by one or more dogs.

Of course, we all know "you can't judge a book by its cover." It's what's on the inside that counts. Unfortunately, by the time a book is replaced, in many cases the information it contains is in even worse shape than the dog-chewed covers holding it together.

Consider a 10-year-old history text. In the summer of 1990, the Commander-in-Chief for the yet-to-be-waged Gulf War was George H. W. Bush, Dick Cheney was the Secretary of Defense, and only one president had been impeached. Science textbooks (no cloning, potential life on Mars or decoded human genome) might be even more dated.

With eBooks, annual—and even daily—updates become possible. Once you have the reader, "all" you have to keep on buying is content. While modern authors don't work as cheaply as the long-deceased Mark Twain, when you don't have to pay for paper, postage or surplus production, the marginal cost of digital data is nearly nil.

Now, some of you are saying, "Egads! That may be true, but books—BOOKS—are special. A page from a book not the same as a screen on a machine!"

True, but consider the REAL shelf life of most books. How long has it been since you picked up the last novel you were assigned to read in high school English? Have you ever—even once—peeked inside a chemistry textbook after you took the final exam?

Also, consider the limitations of pulverized dead trees (another way of saying "book"). Try teaching Mozart without listening to his music, or Martin Luther King without hearing, or seeing, his *I Have a Dream* speech, and suddenly multimedia eBooks seem much more attractive.

Suppose that in several years, if instead of buying textbooks, we were to lease waterproof, "ruggedized" e-readers from the likes of a Barnes and Noble—along with all the content we could conceivably stuff in them—for $50 per student per year. That would give us a figure we could budget for, and keep our technology—and our content—up to date every year, not just once a decade. I could live with that.

Will "real" books ever be retired? I hope not. As I'm typing this, I can see Jack London's *White Fang*, one of the eBooks I downloaded today, sitting in my bookcase. I like the way it looks just sitting there, and how it smells when I crack open its covers. However, there are few timeless books that meet my look and smell test, and when I want one, I can always go the bookstore and buy it, or to the library and borrow it.

For everything else, I'm ready to let my finger do the walking.

CRASH COURSE IN EDUCATIONAL PHILOSOPHY

Some of you might be aware of the unfortunate altercation I had with a sledding hill two winters ago. As you might guess, the hill won.

The day was sunny, children were sliding and smiling, and I was the biggest kid around. On what was to be my "last run of the day," I flew through the air—and landed in the hospital with a broken vertebra.

The healing went well, and in four months I was literally up and running. In the fall, though, an infection invaded the fracture. This time, eight months later, I was just getting so both feet could leave the ground.

Not good enough. I went to the "bone doctor" and "germ doctors" for a remedy. They delivered the best diagnoses modern medicine can provide, but I was still stalled.

It wasn't until I spent time with a TEACHER that I turned the corner. In the process, I came to better appreciate how great teaching, combined with focused instructional time, reliable external data and (quite literally) a motivated student body can profoundly enhance education.

The "teacher" to whom I refer was a physical therapist. PTs are skilled professionals, but work on what's sometimes regarded as a lower rung of the medical ladder than MDs. However, while some otherwise-effective doctors seem to regard their patients as conditions to be cured, therapists succeed only when they maximize the potential of the person before them.

Anyone who's spent time in a hospital, even a "teaching" hospital, knows patient instruction is usually not Job One. It's not anyone's fault. While I tried to learn what I could when residents raced through my room, even during those prime pedagogical moments I was uncomfortable, exhausted, and under the influence of mind-blurring medicines—not quite the student ideal.

Even had I been able to compose coherent questions, my "film" was on far-away floors and my data were on distant computers. Not surprisingly, both times I was discharged, I had general notions of what was done to me, but not much more.

It was in that state of semi-discernment that I finally saw the physical therapist. During my first appointment, there was a short diagnosis and a long teaching session (opposite the usual pattern), during which I learned why things weren't happening and what I could do about it. The meeting convinced me that by paying attention "in class" and doing my homework, I could positively affect my future. Education Lesson One.

Lesson Two, though, was the life-changer. Because I was local, mobile and "interesting," I was asked to appear as a guinea pig/expert eyewitness before a classroom of future physical therapists.

Starting with the sunny day in the snow, we walked through each development, with students offering educated guesses about what happened, and then having their hunches confirmed or corrected by huge zoomed-in images from X-rays and MRIs. I'm sure they learned something, but as the most motivated student in the lecture hall, I was thrilled with the extended opportunity to check out my internal photo album in a rested and upright position, all with the insight of an expert guide.

As an experienced practitioner, the professor probably knew 95 percent of my story before he first laid eyes on me, but even he was sometimes surprised by what he found "going to the video." Similarly, after having my own data explained to me, I not only learned what to do, but why to do it, which can only enhance my odds for success.

Education, like medicine, is both art and science. Sometimes teachers are called to task, fairly or not, for focusing more on the art part, while physicians are more commonly criticized for poring over printouts while ignoring the person in front of them.

In both disciplines, though, I'm convinced there is a sweet spot in the middle, one that took me 16 months to find. Now that I have, my search has become a lesson (along with "Stay off sleds!") in educational philosophy I promise never to forget.

Chapter Four

Extracurricular

THE MUSIC EFFECT

Music, perhaps alone among humanity's creations, has the potential to last forever. Long after our bones have turned to dust, and everything we've built is reduced to rust, our descendants will marvel at the miracle of Mozart, stomp to the Stones, and hold back tears as they sing *Silent Night*.

Yet, despite its unparalleled ability to move us, music is invisible. You can't see it, touch it or taste it, and tragically, in many schools across the country, you can barely even hear it anymore. Arts education is increasingly regarded as a "frill"—something you do if you have extra money lying around which, of course, nobody does. Fortunately, that is NOT the case everywhere.

Earlier this fall, Iowa Music Educators Association bestowed upon Mid-Prairie the *Iowa Exemplary Music Award*, an honor reserved for the one district in the state that has done the most outstanding job of incorporating music in its schools. While we were not granted the same attention we might have had had we won the state football championship, in my mind this was the more meaningful award.

A growing body of evidence suggests an outstanding musical education results in far more than the mastery of tempo, pitch and rhythm. While the "Mozart Effect" (playing Mozart to babies to develop neural pathways among the very young) remains controversial, there is no doubt that musical education enhances skills critical across the curriculum, skills that are equally important throughout one's life.

Harvard University education professor Howard Gardner introduced the idea of "Multiple Intelligences" in his 1983 book, *Frames of Mind*.

at most schools only reward linguistic and logical-mathematical
_____ es"—in other words, reading, writing and arithmetic. While we
focus on these traditional skills, Gardner wrote that there are at least seven
intelligences that we all possess, also including bodily-kinesthetic, spatial,
interpersonal, intrapersonal and musical. Music education obviously tackles
the last intelligence—but also all the others.

A student who can read music has the ability to quickly and accurately
decipher symbols, a linguistic skill that can be put to use reading Shake-
spearean sonnets or pounding out Scott Joplin rags. Kindergartners can
appreciate how properly spaced piano keys combine to create a beautiful
chord (spatial skills), and 2nd graders can grasp how two eighth notes take
the same amount of time to play as a single quarter note—without ever
having to hear the dreaded word *fractions.*

Similarly, bodily-kinesthetic intelligence can be developed by drawing
a bow across a violin, not to mention blowing a horn while strutting across
the field in a marching band. In terms of interpersonal skills, while you
earn normal grades based largely upon how hard you study on your own,
in a band your success depends on every musician working—literally—in
harmony. That's a lesson in teamwork and cooperation that isn't taught in
most classrooms.

As far as "intrapersonal" intelligence is concerned, no one knows more
than a musician does the effort required to excel, and the satisfaction that
comes from achieving excellence. What is particularly gratifying about
music is that one student's success doesn't require the failure of another.
For me to win a basketball game, you must lose it. But if you write a song
that sends chills up my spine, we both benefit from your artistry. That, too,
is a lesson often forgotten in the game of life.

As this century began, Theodore Roosevelt wrote, "Far and away the
best prize that life offers is the chance to work hard at work worth doing."
As the millennium draws to a close, our district has taken that lesson to
heart in the academic discipline that most affects our hearts, and perhaps
even our minds—that of music.

The next time you wonder if our schools are doing a good job of trans-
forming our children into smart, functional and cooperative adults, look in
the paper for the time of our next concert, drive to the school, get a seat
in the front row and listen. Not only will your questions be answered,
chances are your heart will be moved. And if that's not education, I don't
know what is.

REINVENTING THE BOX

"Thinking out of the box" was not only encouraged, but required—and it showed. More than 200 incredible ideas, and enough display-case cardboard to carpet a coliseum, were on display last week at the regional *Invent Iowa* competition. Interspersed among the inventions of some of the finest young minds of eastern Iowa were those of eight Mid-Prairie students. While out of their neighborhood, our kids were not out of their league—but more about that later.

Invent Iowa is designed to get students to look closely at the world around them, find problems that have yet to be addressed, brainstorm solutions, and then act upon their ideas. Once the kids have built their prototypes, they must test them to make sure they work, construct displays that explain their inventions to others, and finally verbalize their solutions to judges.

Our students' work literally spanned the centuries. Julie Zahs, our *Invent Iowa* instructor, confidante and guru, started students looking for ideas in late 1999. Although she had a recent nip-and-tuck on her vocal cords, her unspoken enthusiasm had elementary-aged engineers from across the district toiling away on their ideas throughout the holiday season.

To illustrate the process, I'll take advantage of my 4th-grade son, an *Invent Iowa* contestant. Patrick's friend Josh has neighbor with a cat—and a perennial problem. Each year, the cat knocks over the neighbor's Christmas tree while trying to climb it, a predicament Patrick and Josh set out to resolve.

With Josh's dad keeping watch to ensure they didn't damage their house or each other, the twosome developed the *Animal Ornament Alarm*. The device uses an AA battery, copper wire, a metal nut and a tiny buzzer. When the Christmas tree is still, there's enough clearance between the hanging copper wire and the loop it runs through to keep open an electrical circuit.

However, should the cat climb the tree, the hanging wire—with the heavy metal nut attached to one end—swings back and forth, closing the circuit and setting off the alarm. The entire project required less than a $7 investment in hardware, but it instilled far more information about electricity, drilling, soldering, journal writing and communication than most $70 textbooks.

Other local inventions on display in Cedar Rapids included the *Lean-On-Me* cake decorating platform, *Laundry I-V*, *Handy Stroller Helper*, *Cobra Clip* recipe holder, and the *Everything Chair*.

In the regional competition, I served on a platoon of judges evaluating 45 6th-grade entries. It pleases me to report that the contraptions with the biggest budgets and most elaborate technologies did not fare as well as the simplest, but most elegant, inventions.

In a minor act of civil disobedience, our crew even strayed from the judging criteria to commend a student who clearly had no one helping him make things look pretty. Still, he had constructed his own version of the *Everything Chair* from a cast-off collection of kindling, screws, bent wires and axle grease that would have made Rube Goldberg proud.

Next up for Mid-Prairie's four remaining *Invent Iowa* entries is the state competition. Not only should our students be celebrating, but our community as a whole.

Sometimes there's a tendency for kids in smaller towns to be cowed by their big city peers. The fact is our children can, and should, compete with the best and the brightest anywhere. In addition to learning to drill, solder, and stick with a project until it's done, I hope that's a lesson my son never forgets.

I WANT TO BE A HIGH SCHOOL HERO

This fall I made a life-altering decision for my son without consulting him, or even considering his feelings. When a flier came home seeking recruits for the 5th-grade football team, it was sent straight to the circular file. Through my actions, I probably also trashed any dreams he may have had for gridiron greatness.

It's not that I hate football. As I type this, I'm looking at a photograph of Green Bay Packer quarterback Bart Starr, the Brett Favre of the 1960s. Signed in person at Lambeau Field (*To Jim, A Fine Young American. Best Wishes, Bart Starr*), the photo is perhaps my most prized possession of childhood.

What made me fling the flier is my equally vivid memory of tackling one of my best friends in a backyard game, and seeing him rise from the turf with an obviously broken forearm. I remember thinking, "We're in 5th grade. We're small. We're slow. We're weak. And we're breaking each other's bones. This is only going to get worse."

For me, one broken arm was enough to draw the line—and it wasn't even my arm. Other kids, maybe with more talent, desire or "encouragement," made different decisions, and I'm OK with that. What concerns me are kids who, no matter what the activity, jeopardize their long-term prospects by single-minded devotions to what will undoubtedly be short-term pursuits.

This year, I had a long conversation with another local parent. He had enjoyed a successful high school sporting career, but realized soon after graduation that devoting more time to doing his homework might have paid greater dividends in the game of life than spending all those hours bouncing, hitting and throwing balls.

It is possible, of course, to be a great student-athlete, but reaching that plateau requires rare discipline, and a culture that recognizes both goals as important. While such students are uncommon, I suspect such cultures are even harder to find.

In 1998, I attended my 20th high school reunion. Like everyone else, I searched the walls for photos of people I knew. While we had national-class debate and journalism programs, in addition to a class president, valedictorian and other academic luminaries, the only familiar faces belonged to a handful of our best athletes.

As a board member for my former district once pointed out, a school's walls literally speak to you. They too often say, "This is what we honor, and these are the people we revere. At our school, immortality is achieved through athletic greatness." Even then, try parlaying that limited glory into success in college or a career, or as a wife, husband, parent or citizen. My read of the class of 1978 is that our "famous few" didn't score any higher in those measures than our less-celebrated multitudes.

Is this a condemnation of athletics? No. It's a critique of any activity that, when taken to an extreme, forecloses other opportunities. Ron Borges, a Boston sportswriter, knows America's greatest athletes better than any of us ever will. This is what he had to say after a recent Dallas Cowboy's football game:

> Quarterback Troy Aikman ended up with the ninth concussion of his career, more than most boxers would be allowed to take and keep on fighting. . . . Each time his head goes dark, it takes less of a hit to do it. It's what drove Steve Young out of football. It's what left former Jets' wide receiver Al Toon sometimes forgetting the names of his own children years after he stopped playing. It's not pretty to watch.
>
> This is no lament for today's professional football player because he has made a choice. He is not a Christian being thrown to the lions after becoming

a slave. He is a volunteer who has decided it is worth the risk to put his body
on the line each week because the rewards are big and the adulation bigger.

As adults, it's our obligation to make sure our children are not slaves to
high school's highest currency, the adulation of friends and even teachers.
I met a former math teacher of mine a few years back. He couldn't remember me, but he could name the starting five from our basketball team.
Remind me again what high school's about?

Students should enjoy extracurricular activities for what they are—
opportunities to develop specific talents, and generalized skills such as
perseverance, self-discipline and teamwork. It's another supposed
virtue, "sacrifice," that I worry about. A picture on the wall may be
worth a fracture, but it's not worth a future.

By the way, after it was too late to do anything about it, I confessed to
my son about tossing out his football application. Patrick, perhaps realiz-
ing half his genes came from me, said "Not a problem."

Good call.

THE ALFORD-HANSEN SCHOOL OF EMPATHY

Not long ago, I worried more about Luke Recker's head than his knee.
The University of Iowa basketball star had been limping for a month, even
though his X-rays came up clean.

When Recker sat out a game, coach Steve Alford said Indiana's Mr.
Basketball was welcome to return when he decided he liked playing more
than watching. Bobby Hansen told his radio audience how his NBA coach
would have handled Recker's tendonitis— "Luke, get an aspirin, tape it to
your knee and get back in the game."

It was only after his heroic efforts against Indiana, in which Recker
poured in 27 points despite breaking his kneecap early in the contest, that
the doubts about his head and knee were laid to rest (along with, unfortunately, the rest of the Hawkeye season).

The point? Great athletes don't let discomfort derail their dreams, great
coaches push their players to perform—and sometimes there really is
something wrong.

David Drew, dean of the Claremont School of Educational Studies, also comes from the Alford-Hansen School of Empathy. He describes African American college students who struggled with calculus while their Chinese classmates excelled. The explanation was that the black kids came from impoverished homes and schools, and therefore shouldn't be expected to succeed.

Not content to merely document the discrepancy, Drew and his colleagues did something about it. They started a workshop replicating Chinese study habits—including doing more homework than was assigned and studying in groups. As you might guess, the black students outperformed their Anglo and Asian peers—destroying the theory that they didn't have the advantages (or worse, the "aptitude") necessary to succeed.

This isn't just an ethnic issue. Drew found that superb female math students—those in the top 10 percent—didn't see themselves that way. More than three-fourths who met that criterion didn't believe it to be true.

If people tend to gravitate toward their perceived talents, chances are these women will shy away from their actual abilities. This self-imposed prejudice, nurtured by the semi-subliminal drumbeat, "Girls aren't good at math," closes doors to learning and to lucrative math-dependent careers such as engineering and computer science.

In our recent reports on local student achievement, it was noted that our minimum graduation requirements have stiffened considerably, and that our college-level courses quadrupled, in the past several years.

Still, Mid-Prairie's mean ACT score is 21.8 (about Iowa's average), while Mount Vernon's is 26—with NO advanced placement classes to jumpstart their scores. What's up with that?

Considering that M-P's kids and curriculum are at least M-V's equals, that seems to leave Cornell College as the likely culprit.

My guess is Cornell contributes a critical mass of children to Mount Vernon classrooms from families that have learned how to achieve academic success. Other kids don't see these "faculty brats" as anything special, because they aren't.

Nonetheless, M-V's kids measure themselves against this elevated standard. The result is a self-reinforcing cycle of high expectations and performance, which Mount Vernon didn't create, but from which it certainly benefits.

How do we get similar results? Perhaps, in part, by employing lessons from the Alford-Hansen School of Empathy. It didn't work for Iowa this year, but Iowa State's Larry Eustachy used it to win his second straight Big 12 title.

Entering this season, Eustachy had lost the best player in ISU history, Marcus Fizer. Instead of complaining, he worked the players he had left to the limits of their talent. It wasn't always pretty.

According to Kantrail Horton, "Coach Eustachy and his staff taught us to be men, on and off the court. Some players couldn't take what we went through, but our name for that is 'Tough Love.'" Eustachy adds, "They have always known I wanted what's best for them. These guys will do anything for me, and they know I'd do anything for them. That's what counts."

Mid-Prairie doesn't have to "beat" Mount Vernon or anybody else to prove its academic worth. At the same time, we must never be afraid to remind our students that learning, like winning, is often hard work—but that those who can tolerate temporary discomforts will be permanently rewarded.

That's true in basketball, in calculus and, most importantly, in life.

So, find an aspirin, tape it to your forehead, and get out there and study!

MORE THAN AN ACADEMIC EXERCISE

During the spring of 1970, discontent permeated the nation. Close to home, anti-war demonstrations shook the University of Iowa, windows were being shattered daily in downtown Iowa City, and at Ernest Horn Elementary School, my alma mater, the feud between the "City Slicks" and the "Country Hicks" was coming to a head.

Each day after lunch, the "Hicks"—who rode buses and ate at school—staked out their claims to the playground equipment. The "Slicks"—who walked and ate at home for lunch—were left to watch their mostly country cousins play away once they finally returned.

After several weeks of simmering resentment, the situation came to a head. Like pint-sized replicas of the Sharks and the Jets, the two factions decided to resolve their differences with a rumble—or more specifically, a winner-take-all game of dodgeball.

For the uninitiated, dodgeball is a brutally simple game in which two teams attempt to annihilate each other with a red playground ball. If you hit a player on the other team with a thrown ball, he's out of the game—unless he catches your throw, in which case you're "dead" and one of his teammates returns to life. When one team wipes out the other, it wins.

I don't recall much of 5th grade, but I do remember that just as the schoolyard skirmish started, our principal, Mr. Delozier, sprinted out Horn's back entrance, stepped between the two hostile factions, mandated an immediate cease fire, and ultimately returned peace to the playground.

Clearly, what happens outside the classroom can be critical to a school's educational environment. This week, we learned about elements of our curriculum that don't often get much attention—health and physical education.

In contrast to my P-E classes, which seemed heavy on dodgeball (yes, the teachers taught us that game), flag football and square dancing, activities I haven't participated in since high school, the first goal of our health curriculum is "to develop personal responsibility for lifelong health."

A glance at the "scope and sequence" of the program proves the point. In the 7th and 8th grades, for example, classrooms explore cholesterol, refusal skills, fetal alcohol syndrome and the Heimlich Maneuver. By high school, discussions expand to include mental health and *Maslow's Hierarchy of Needs*—good stuff I never got in high school.

However, it's when the kids switch out of street clothes and into gym shorts that the biggest changes become clear. In addition to pull-ups, sit-ups and shuttle runs, today's kids learn about aerobics, boating and biking safety, power walking, orienteering, yoga, roller skating and fishing—things real people actually do after leaving high school.

The development of an appropriate P-E curriculum is more than just an "academic exercise." This month, the National Center on Health Statistics released a study that found that while 5 percent of 6–11-year-olds were overweight in 1970, 13.6 percent were too heavy by 1994. Chubbier children are at a higher risk for developing diabetes and high blood pressure as youngsters, and are more likely to be overweight when they grow up—a condition that already afflicts more than half of all American adults.

Schools can't make kids push themselves away from the TV, but they are finding that if they can push students to literally work up a sweat at school, the dividends don't end with lower cholesterol counts—they also mean higher test scores.

Carl Gabbard, a Texas A&M professor of health and kinesiology and president of the National Association for Sport and Physical Education, states flatly that "Children who are physically fit do better in school. That's a statement we can make. Physical activity doesn't make students smarter, but they're more alert and can concentrate better. That we know."

In short, time spent on the monkey bars isn't just monkey business.

Thirty years ago, the "Slicks" and the "Hicks" learned some valuable lessons on the Ernest Horn playground. As this new century begins, let's hope for a happy medium in which a solid foundation in lifelong learning about health and physical education literally translates into longer lives for our children.

A LANDMARK CLASS

Mid-Prairie Senior High School has graduated its Class of 2000, a group of young men and women who knew, literally from the day they started school, they were something special.

Four seniors—Lindsey Yoder, Kendra Johnson, Lucas Grout and Michael Huston—addressed their peers during the ceremony, which saw 67 students receive their diplomas. The following is a composite of their speeches, and should serve as a comfort to all those who care about our future.

Lindsey: We all started our first day of kindergarten the same, whether it was at Wellman, Kalona, Washington Township or some other school. We had been told that we were the Class of 2000, and that we were going to make a difference. I don't think anyone of us really knew what that meant. We were just glad to know we were going to have naptime and snacktime.

Kendra: Each and every one of us walked into a kindergarten classroom clutching our parents' hands, wanting them to stay there right beside us, not leaving us alone. But they weren't really leaving us alone. They were starting us out and guiding us on a path we would follow the next 13 years.

Lucas: I remember we got our picture in the paper for being "The Class of 2000." They even made little shirts that had "Class of 2000, Last Class of the Century" on them. Back in kindergarten, it seemed like it would be forever before we would actually graduate. Heck, some people even said the world would end before we graduated. Now, how could the world end without ME graduating?

Michael: We were going to be like Peter Pan and be kids forever, or so we thought. The future was something that was as far away as the next milk break, recess, or weekend slumber party at a friend's house.

Lindsey: (As we entered junior high), something great happened. We realized we were even better with the three elementaries combining. People began making new friends, keeping the old and expanding horizons. Soon everyone realized it didn't matter what town you were from or how popular you used to be. This was a whole new ballgame.

Michael: We became closer to our friends over these past few years than we ever thought imaginable. On more than one occasion, we discovered who our true friends were. They were the ones who were there for us, no matter how big or how small the situation. As the days before graduation grew nearer, we realized they were what we would miss most about high school.

Lindsey: At the beginning of this year, we kept saying, "I can't wait till I get out of here." But in the back of our minds, we were all secretly praying we would never leave. The volleyball girls burst into tears as the last point of their last game was scored. All of us girls waited for the guys after their final football game at Clear Creek Amana, just like every other game. Only this wasn't like every other game. It was the last one of their high school careers. Many of us had never seen them cry before, but now it didn't matter who was the toughest.

Kendra: In elementary, we turned to our parents for everything, from a minor scratch to a broken bone. In junior high, we thought we knew everything and our parents knew nothing. But we were soon to learn that we knew nothing and they knew everything. And now we're turning to them again to help us with decisions that will shape our lives forever.

Lucas: "I will not follow where the path may lead, but I will go where there is no path, and I will leave a trail." As we leave here today, let us all look back at the paths that we have traveled and let us see the trails that we have left behind.

Michael: We didn't follow in the footsteps of the classes before us. We broke away from the path and made our own trail. Always follow your dreams and don't ever forget your past.

Lindsey: Whether you choose to go to college or start right off with a career, know that you can and will accomplish anything you put your minds to. We have been through many hardships and many high spots, but we have grown tremendously from these experiences. Even though this sounds like the end, it isn't. We have only begun.

A TEAM FOR THE AGES

Sports fans tend to be numerologists, and Mid-Prairie's girls basketball team posted numbers this season that will stand the test of time: 28–0, No. 1, and 3.74.

The first two figures are well known—their 28–0 record, and their No. 1 finish in the state (and conference) basketball standings.

The third figure, though, is what we—and especially they—should be most proud of. It's the TEAM grade point average, earned during a physically and emotionally exhausting season. That all-star performance should prove, once and for all, that kids who can execute X's and O's on the court can also understand X's and Y's in the classroom.

This is not just a feel-good story for Mid-Prairie. It's one the Iowa Board of Education should study as it considers revising the state's athletic eligibility rules.

Next month, the board may insist athletes earn at least a 2.0 GPA if they want to play ball, and perhaps pass all their classes. Current rules only require passing four classes with grades of D-minus or higher. A third of some schools' athletes wouldn't meet the stiffer standards—and hundreds would fail the test statewide.

According to board member Gregory McClain, as quoted in the *Des Moines Register*, "It's embarrassing and hypocritical for us to say from one side of our mouth 'higher academic achievement' and on the other side say it's OK for members of our sports teams to get D's and F's."

A survey of superintendents, teachers and coaches, though, found that most oppose raising the academic bar. They believe kids who can't compete will drop out, become disciplinary problems, avoid challenging classes, or benefit from grading standards that might become—shall we say—somewhat less stringent than Mid-Prairie's full-court press.

In my mind, though, those arguments are trumped by the term schools use to describe their players—*student-athlete*. A student who can't pull a C average probably needs to spend less time launching lay-ups and more time writing essays. If the classes they're considering are truly too hard to pass even with an honest effort, that's a failure of academic advising; they should be enrolled in courses where they have a chance for success and a prospect for learning.

If we're worried about kids becoming truants or troublemakers because their classes are too demanding, most coaches don't lose sleep over practices that make kids exert themselves. Coaches know winners must "give 110 percent." The athletes do too, and often welcome authority figures that insist they live up to their potential.

Coddling athletes doesn't do them any favors. Just ask Kevin Ross, the subject of a recent ESPN documentary. Ross attended Creighton University from 1978 to 1982—the same years I went to Macalester College. The biggest difference was that Creighton expected him to win basketball games—and Macalester expected me to pass tests.

As a result, I survived four years at Mac despite being unable to dunk, and Ross survived four years at Creighton despite being unable to read. Ross was, it was later discovered, functionally illiterate. I suspect his college experience might have been more rewarding had more adults cared as much about his reading as they did his rebounding.

Last week, I received a letter from Macalester's current athletic director, Irv Cross (former NFL cornerback and TV announcer). Mac announced it's leaving the football conference in which it's been overmatched for years (it set a record for consecutive losses—51—during my time), but it's keeping its team and its ideals.

In his letter, Cross wrote "Along with physical skills, student-athletes gain self-confidence, a sense of team play and leadership that make them more complete people and more productive in whatever career they choose. . . . That, helping students develop and grow, is our strength, and everything we do should reflect that strength."

At some point (far in the future), Mid-Prairie won't win the state title, but this year's girls will always be champions—because they prepared themselves for success in whatever endeavors they'll choose in life, most of which won't involve jump shots.

For diminutive dribblers looking up to these girls as heroes, in addition to 28–0, they should also remember 3.74. Records are made to be broken, and I hope someday (in the not-so-distant future) this team's record is topped by the next generation of outstanding student-athletes.

FATHER GOOSE ON THE LOOSE:
AN AMATEUR POET TACKLES PROSE

From time to time, a frustrated parent laments
On the course of modern scholastic events

"When I went to school we were smart and worked hard!
Today's kids can't tell Dr. Seuss from the Bard!"

Mid-Prairie, I know, is hardly immune
From complaints that seem somewhat jejune
But the truth, I concede, is that it's our job to lead
The effort to teach our kids how to read

To that end, I submit, we've warmed up to the task
How? (Assuming you elected to ask)
With Read-a-thons, Book-Its, and *One Million Minutes*
All programs that should start to silence the cynics

We bring in mayors, seniors and community leaders
To share cherished stories with our budding young readers
And should second graders think these are old "fuddy-duddies"
They've also been paired with fifth-grade *Reading Buddies*

Why so fanatically committed to reading?
It's the research, my friend, we're dedicated to heeding
It's readers who graduate! The stats couldn't be clearer
And for the help we need? Well, just look in the mirror

With spring semester near settled, soon will come summer
But I pray that with school out, our kids don't get no dumber
Vacations are intended to give breaks to the brain
But why not interrupt MTV with a little Mark Twain?

At the pool, I know, there are tans to be won
But books do quite well when lit up by the sun
And yes, I'm aware, muscles must sometimes be flexed
But biceps look fine when toting a text

And if it rains, don't pout, be sad or contrary
Just visit the climate-controlled local library!
The drops can go on overflowing the gauges
If you're inside, warm and dry, with the wisdom of ages

Indoors or outdoors, you won't have to grovel
For something to do when your hands hold a novel

It may be a romance, a comedy or mystery
And for the serious among us, there's science and history

Pick what you want! There are no strictures!
Look for wonderful writing or heavenly pictures!
Iowa has loads of pigs and chickens and cows and...
If you're looking for books, we have them by the thousands

Yes, summer comes soon, but it will be gone in a blink
Why not share some of those hours with great paper and ink?
Whether your name is Yoder, Hussey, Hochstetler or Zook
Just sit back, relax, and crack open a book!

Chapter Five

Teachers

WE'RE TOO BUSY TO WATCH MOVIES

In the last few days, football changed in the United States—and in Iowa—forever. Tom Landry, the Dallas Cowboys coach despised by many in life, died to universal sorrow at the age of 75. Meanwhile, Reese Morgan, the coach who transformed Iowa City West from the state's worst football team to its best, resigned his high school post to work at the University of Iowa.

Both men achieved unparalleled success. Landry was Dallas's first, and for 29 years its only, head coach. He won 270 games and two Super Bowls before being unceremoniously fired by new owner Jerry Jones in 1989. Known for wearing a business suit and fedora along the sidelines, he led his team not so much with words as with expectations. You never heard Landry berate his players, or have a temper tantrum when a call didn't go his way. Most years, you only saw him win.

In 1992, Morgan took over a football team that had lost 32 straight games, and turned the program around on a dime. Over the last five years, West has won 53 of its 56 games, and three class 4A titles—including the last two. Like Landry, Morgan said his success didn't result from the genius of one man, but rather the soundness of his "system." His players agreed. Although there were many tears at West last Wednesday, there was also an expectation of continued excellence in Morgan's absence. Nate Kaeding, who will punt for the Hawkeyes next year, said "Nobody should be disappointed by what happened, because the program's great."

Landry and Morgan succeeded in creating cultures of excellence. Their players knew that if they wanted to be a Cowboy or a Trojan, they had to be in the shape of their lives, give it their all every practice, memorize their playbooks, and play with the focused abandon that wins football games.

The manner in which ideas transform cultures is the subject of Malcolm Gladwell's new book, *The Tipping Point*. According to a review in *Time*, "Every notion and product can catch on in ways that resemble medical contagions. The most explosive are set off when very effective carriers spread very potent strains in very conducive settings. And in these social outbursts, Gladwell tells us, small things have big consequences."

The most famous example is the "Broken Window Theory" propounded by New York City police commissioner William Bratton. He argues that if you want to stop rapes, robberies and murders, you must first fight litter, graffiti and broken windows. By tolerating small signs of decay, society creates an environment in which worse crimes can flourish. New York City's remarkable turnaround under Bratton, like the football Trojans under Morgan, is evidence of the merits of this argument.

Instilling a culture of excellence is something that is both incredibly hard, and at the same time, almost remarkably easy. My daughter is a 2nd grader. At the beginning of this school year, she and several classmates approached their teacher, Kerri Bell, and asked if they could watch a movie. Mrs. Bell had a simple answer—"We're too busy in this classroom to watch movies. We've got important things to do."

Molly has forgotten the movie they wanted to watch, but she hasn't forgotten the answer. Mrs. Bell's insistence upon excellence—like Bratton's, Morgan's and Landry's—shows up in the quality of the schoolwork Molly brings home every Friday, and in the lessons she'll carry with her the rest of her life.

Many people didn't care for Tom Landry when he coached *America's Team,* but after he left the field, their opinions changed. A Louisiana man recalls watching Landry's *Ring of Honor* induction in 1993 in a tavern filled with "Cowboy haters."

> At halftime, a frightful hush fell over the entire bar. You could have heard a pin drop. Everybody was glued to the television set and the man wearing the hat. At the completion of the induction ceremony, I looked at my teary eyed friend and said, "I wouldn't have believed this if I had not been here to see it." America will surely miss Tom Landry.

It doesn't take many words to send a powerful message. Tom Landry proved that throughout his three decades with the Cowboys, Reese Morgan proved that during his eight years at Iowa City West, and Kerri Bell proves that every day in her 2nd-grade classroom. While our wins and losses tend to be noticed in the short term, it's the lives we lead and standards we set that are remembered.

MEASURE A KID WITH NUMBERS?

Think of the people you care most about. Could you adequately describe them with a page of numbers, a dozen charts, or even an encyclopedia's worth of words? I hope not.

Despite the difficulties, Mid-Prairie High School's staff and faculty have prepared an outstanding report describing several hundred kids they care deeply about—their students. Going beyond test scores and course grades, the 38-page document gets at what makes us tick, and lays the groundwork for further analysis in the years to come.

The report's first measures are the "easy" ones—standardized test scores. While seemingly straightforward, as Principal Gerry Beeler explained at a parents' meeting last week, numbers are only useful if they're viewed in context.

For example, Mid-Prairie's ACT Assessment scores have been trending upward for 12 years (disclosure: I work for ACT). With a 21.8 composite score, they're a full point above the national mean, but 0.2 points under the state average.

Should M-P kids rank higher within Iowa? Not necessarily. If that was our only goal, we could accomplish it overnight by discouraging our weaker kids from testing. With them out of the picture, our average scores would shoot up, and we'd immediately be "better" than the rest of the state.

Would we have improved the quality of our instruction? Of course not. To our credit, M-P pushes as many kids as possible to take the ACT, which hurts our scores but helps our kids—which is what education is all about.

Other data are easier to deconstruct. Take our Advanced Placement classes. These courses can result in college credit if students reach certain levels on nationally administered final examinations.

From 8 in 1996, our A-P enrollment has skyrocketed to 53 this year. Our A-P curriculum has also grown from one to four classes, and now includes English, Biology, Chemistry and Calculus (with History in the works).

It's hard to argue with the quality of this instruction, but some do. They suggest A-P courses are great for "high-end" students, but worry about the kids who may end their formal educations at MPHS.

Well, for one thing, we're making sure these students spend more time in class while they're here. Our graduation requirements have risen from 42 credit hours in 1998 to 52.5 this year (and 56 next year). For kids doing the minimum to get by, that means a third more work is required to receive a Mid-Prairie diploma.

Not only do kids have less leisure time by district dictate, they're also spending more "time on task" by choice. Our attendance rate reached 95.3 percent in 2000, about as high as high schools get. It may be that fewer flus are passing through, but it's more likely that kids are simply deciding they don't want to miss school.

Of course, for some students, that isn't a choice; they've been suspended. However, the way they "serve their time" has also changed markedly over the past half decade. In 1996, 31 kids served out-of-school suspensions. This year, only one has. If you're a kid angry at the world, would you rather "suffer" the "penalty" of mandatory hooky, or be forced to confront your problems within the confines of MPHS? It's almost enough make you straighten up and fly right.

In fact, the data suggest that's exactly what's happening. Fights (one this year) are at near-historic lows, "disrespect to faculty" has declined from 10 incidents most years to none this year, and in-school suspensions have dropped from 73 in 1996 to 31.

Perhaps the only discouraging number related to the report was the turnout at the parent meeting itself, particularly when compared to the crowd packing the gym one floor below. Presentations on student achievement don't draw the same swarms as district playoff basketball games, and probably never will. Still, that evening's information described in detail people we all care deeply about—our students.

As we work on our Comprehensive School Improvement Plan, and as we prepare for next year's visits of our accreditors, I hope we can get as demonstrably excited about what happens in our classrooms as on our basketball courts.

In the meantime, our faculty and staff deserve a standing ovation for posting some outstanding numbers on our scholastic scoreboard, as do the students these data valiantly attempt to describe.

AND THE WINNER IS . . .

Quick! Name the American university that has won 61 national athletic titles in the last 20 years, with 13 different coaches. Michigan? Notre Dame? Nope—try again.

Last year, its teams won PAC-10 titles in football, men's basketball and baseball (and the national title in track), the first to win all three in the same year. UCLA? USC? Wrong!

More hints? In 1996, its students won 16 gold and 23 total medals at the Atlanta Olympics (seven more than England!). This year, it has 34 athletes and coaches in Sydney.

Still don't have it? One last chance. This university also boasts of 12 Nobel laureates, four Supreme Court justices, and of being the birthplace of the Internet revolution.

That's right. Stanford University. Arguably our most influential academic institution, Stanford has also been voted home of the nation's top athletic program six years running.

How does Stanford do it? Its athletic director claims the secret is simply having "big, hairy, audacious goals," and following through on them. According to Ted Elder, as quoted in *USA Today*, "Our goal is to be the most dominant athletic program in the history of college athletics. We don't say that publicly, but we do say it internally."

Closer to home, there also seems to be an aspiring Stanford. Last year, Iowa City West (I admit, my alma mater) won state football, basketball and soccer championships, and trumped that trifecta by producing 20 National Merit Scholarship semifinalists last year and 18 more this year—the most in Iowa, and six times the number expected of a school its size.

Principal Jerry Arganbright says four factors contribute to that record: quality teachers, hard-working students, a challenging curriculum, and "The instructional culture of our school is that we are always looking to do something better."

Mid-Prairie also has excellent teachers and students, but like every other school in Iowa, I don't think we can claim West's success. Should we care? Maybe not.

According to 19th-century educator William Graham Sumner, "We throw all our attention on the utterly idle question whether A has done as well as B, when the only question is whether A has done as well as he could."

Then again, in the words of a second serious thinker, Ovid, who lived at the time of Christ, "A horse never runs so fast as when he has other horses to catch up and outpace."

Whether or not we want to outpace anyone else, how hard should we ask ourselves to run? I suggest we try these three goals on for size:

- Each year, Mid-Prairie will produce at least one National Merit Scholar.
- Each year, Mid-Prairie will win at least one extracurricular state championship
- Each year, 90 percent of Mid-Prairie's students will read and do math at the proficient level or above.

To achieve those goals, we must provide a rock-solid academic and extracurricular foundation for all our students, and must create a culture that almost forces our most talented students to achieve at the highest possible levels.

Does that seem too big, hairy or audacious to you? I hope not. For a school our size to produce National Merit Scholars at the pace of Iowa City West, we'd be churning out three winners each year, not just the initial goal of one. If you really want audacious, check out three of Stanford's current athletic goals, which include:

- Having all its varsity teams ranked in the top 20 nationally.
- Winning 25 national or NCAA titles in the next four years.
- Winning national championships in five sports that they haven't won before.

That's not just audacious, it's obnoxious—but that's not all bad either. As a third philosopher, Ralph Waldo Emerson, wrote more than one hundred years ago, "Every child of the Saxon race is educated to wish to be first. It is our system; and a man comes to measure his greatness by the regrets, envies and hatreds of his competitors."

If we set audacious enough goals and follow through on them, five years from now, when people start rattling off statistics describing Iowa's (or the nation's) best small-school academic and extracurricular program, the answer could be—and should be—"Mid-Prairie."

And, if that results in the "envies or hatreds of our competitors," bring it on.

ALL MUST HAVE PRIZES

In Iowa, we're supposed to loathe Minnesota, but who can help but love Garrison Keillor's mythical Lake Wobegon, where "the women are strong, the men are good looking, and all the children are above average"?

Actually, Iowa is a lot like Lake Wobegon, at least when it comes to our kids. For example, Mid-Prairie's fall grades just came out. While the average 9th grader compiled a solid 2.93 grade point average (almost a B), the seniors posted a spectacular 3.34 class GPA.

Should we be pleased by such a stellar performance? I hate to be the skunk at the garden party, but I'm troubled by such apparent excellence.

Why? Look at the numbers. For two dozen hypothetical students to earn a 3.33 GPA, a distribution that makes the numbers work is 14 As, 7 Bs, 1 C, 1 D and 1 F. If you assume a couple kids are barely there, to reach a B+ class average the rest must earn As and a few Bs. If you assume every student is right on target, you get 8 As and 16 Bs—and no Cs, Ds, or Fs.

This trend toward higher grades is not just a local phenomenon. Where I work (ACT), we tend to regard the SAT the same way Iowa does Minnesota. Nonetheless, recent college board research found that SAT "test takers with A averages grew from 28 percent of the total to 38 percent in the last 10 years—but their scores fell an average of 12 points on the verbal portion of the SAT and three points on math."

Stephen Landsbury, author of *Why Grade Inflation is Bad for Schools—and What to Do about It*, writes that at the college level, many professors "take a special interest in their own students and . . . give those students a boost at the expense of the anonymous strangers who signed up for someone else's class. Besides, easy graders are more popular on campus. The costs of leniency—measured in lost reputation—are spread over the entire school, while the benefits are concentrated in the professor's own classroom."

Many educators, of course, argue for the deemphasis or outright elimination of grades. As a one-semester student at College of the Atlantic in Bar Harbor, Maine, a school small enough for each professor to write an essay on each student for each class, I can attest to the value of these more nuanced evaluations—but I also asked for optional letter grades because I wasn't sure how potential employers or graduate schools might react to a stack of essays substituting for one transcript with one composite GPA.

Of course, if most students receive As, the only way to get real data from a transcript is to move to an essay grading format in our schools (yeah, right), or rely even more on standardized tests, a prospect that would make many grade-hating educators recoil in horror.

Aside from my one semester in Maine, I was an economics major at Macalester College in loathsome Minnesota. During that era at Mac, I discovered 15 percent of all economics grades were As, in contrast to 42 percent in psychology. That meant in an economics class of 24 students, 3 or 4 earned As, and the rest fought over table scraps.

To combat the odds, two friends and I formed a study group, and beat economics into our skulls for hours on end. We often earned A's in the short term, but in the more important long term, we turned out to be an economics professor, an executive at an international financial services firm, and (last and least) a guy who donates modestly interesting columns to the national conversation on education.

Would we have studied as hard if we were psych students, whom we derided as "having A's until proven guilty"? Not a chance. Although we loved economics (yes, that is possible), we also enjoyed the other pursuits that occasionally accompany college life.

Garrison Keillor may think today's kids are all above average, but in *Alice's Adventures in Wonderland*, Lewis Carroll described a race that suggests this was also true centuries ago. When the race was over, the runners asked a Dodo who had won.

"This question the Dodo could not answer without a great deal of thought, and it sat for a long time with one finger pressed upon its forehead. . . . At last the Dodo said, 'Everybody has won, and all must have prizes.'"

Yippee.

HE JUMPS! HE SHOOTS! HE SCORES?

Imagine you're a basketball scout, and your job is to evaluate an unknown team—but under a very limited set of conditions. You do not know the team's win–loss record, and you cannot ask. Instead, you must evaluate each of the team's players on an individual basis, and everything you want to know about them must be answered by two numbers written on one piece of paper.

As a scout, you'd like to gauge the players' determination, but you can't. No one knows how to quantify a player's heart. You'd like to measure leadership, but again, you're stuck. How do you measure the intangibles that turn five individuals into a "team"?

So, you measure what you can quantify. You settle on "vertical jump" (how high a player can leap) and "free throw percentage" (the proportion of shots an unguarded player makes 15 feet from the basket). While limited, these measurements mean the same thing from player to player, and aren't susceptible to evaluator prejudice. While not the whole story, you're more impressed by teams that play above the rim and can shoot lights out than those that can't—even though you'd also like to know their height, quickness, and ability to execute the pick-and-roll.

Now, imagine you're charged with evaluating a student, a school or a district. You're limited to two mathematical measurements so, like the basketball scout, you focus on what you can quantify.

In education, those measurements tend to be standardized tests. Students who earn high marks for math and reading on the *Iowa Test of Basic Skills*, the *ACT Assessment* or *Scholastic Assessment Test* tend to do better in school than those who don't. To get a true measure, though, you'd also like to be able to look at determination, emotional resilience and teachability— characteristics that mean as much or more in the game of life than scores on standardized tests.

As a whole, our students do well on standardized tests. The percentages earning "proficient or above" scores in reading and math vary by grade and discipline, but can be up to 15 percentage points more than their state peers, and in no subject or grade do we demonstrate an appreciable deficit.

Standardized scores can tell something about students and the school districts they belong to—but you're kidding yourself if you think they tell you everything there is to know. Look at your child or grandchild, or any youngster you love. It's insulting to think they can be fairly represented by two numbers on a piece of paper, yet somehow we expect test scores to tell us exactly how well our students and schools are performing.

Each child, like each of us, is a jumbled collection of strengths and weaknesses. It's the way these characteristics interact that will ultimately determine success in life (and try, for just a moment, to quantify that). Our schools' job is to sort through the jumble so that over time, our kids can grow to be successful adults, however you define "success."

Basketball scouts must predict how five players will behave on climate-controlled 94-foot floors over the course of 40-minute games—and know their efforts are educated guesses at best. Mid-Prairie schools are charged not only with predicting, but preparing 1,250 children for success in a constantly changing global environment over the course of what might be 94-year lifetimes.

Like a good basketball team, our school district wins a lot and loses a few. If we are to make the most of our potential, we must have kids who play with all their hearts, teachers who evaluate their coaching skills through the success of their students, and passionate fans (you) who actively support the team.

That's not an insurmountable task. We do it for basketball. We should do no less in the game of life.

IOWA THE IRRESPONSIBLE

Irresponsible. It's not a pleasant word, but it's the one the Thomas B. Fordham Foundation uses to describe Iowa's educational standards. The foundation's leaders are convinced tough standards, combined with equally tough penalties for nonperforming students and educators, are the secret to school success. Unfortunately, according to a report released earlier this month by the foundation, Iowa and 20 other states "cannot claim to embrace standards-based reform."

As Iowans, should we be ashamed of our spot on Fordham's skid row— or proud? One clue may be the five states placed on the foundation's "honor roll"—Alabama, California, North Carolina, South Carolina and Texas. Would you rather have your child attending school in one of these paragons of pedagogical performance, or going to class in one of our equally "irresponsible" sister states? Hint—the "bad" list also includes Minnesota, North Dakota, Oregon and Vermont.

While statewide standards may or may not be useful, it's obvious from Fordham's own lists that you cannot pass laws that automatically result in academic achievement. When actual learning is measured (as by the National Assessment of Educational Progress), the five states on the Fordham "honor roll" are towards the tail end of the curve, and the "irresponsible" states are generally setting the standards for everyone else.

These counterintuitive findings show just how hard it is to link external standards to what goes on within a student's mind. Acknowledging that reality, Iowa—alone among the 50 states—has consciously decided not only to be "irresponsible," but also to not even play the game.

Instead of dictating what appropriate achievement ought to be, the Iowa Department of Education has delegated that responsibility to local school districts. Perhaps in an example of "be careful what you wish for," educators who might normally resent the heavy hand of the state are now struggling with the yeoman task of measuring their schools with self-designed yardsticks.

This month, several Mid-Prairie board members received instruction in *Chapter 12—General Accreditation Standards* of the *Iowa Administrative Code—School Rules of Iowa*. The bottom line? While we may not have to do exactly what Des Moines tells us, we have to do something—actually, lots of things. According to just the 44 pages of code we received at the meeting, our board must appoint a school improvement advisory committee, adopt long-range goals, write a comprehensive school improvement plan, and collect and analyze the data necessary to judge our schools' performance.

In most larger districts, there are well-paid professionals whose jobs are to manage slices of the curriculum. We don't have the luxury of delegating the heavy lifting to anonymous administrators and, in my mind, we're better off for it. If we really believe in local control of our schools, it means all of us—staff, students, parents, board members and community supporters—need to be involved.

As an administrator for the University of Alaska, I had the "privilege" of chairing my community college's accreditation self-study, along with the duties of my regular job. If the result of our collective two years' work had just been a 300-page report that ended up on some bureaucrat's shelf, the self-study would have been a colossal waste of time. Instead, because every employee and student of our college was involved, as well as people from all segments of our communities, the self-study helped us figure out what we were about, and what we wanted to become.

Our principals have taken the lead in working with their staffs to determine what standards make sense for their students. I can only applaud their efforts, because I know how much work is involved. While I may be "talking out of school," if you want a voice in shaping our schools' future, this is your chance to make a difference. Visit with your principal, talk to your teacher, call the central office or show up at a board meeting, and find out how your voice can be heard because, by law, it must be.

Are Iowa schools "irresponsible"? The answer is obviously "No." In fact, if the proof is in the pudding, most states would do well to copy our recipe for success. Nonetheless, continued excellence requires continued commitment, from all of us.

Like it or not, that is our responsibility.

MOVING THE NEEDLE

Every so often, it's easy to wonder if hard work makes a difference. You go on a diet, but excess pounds stay plastered in place. You clean your house top to bottom, and a week later it's a disaster. You try your best, but you just can't seem to win.

It's no different in education. For a generation or more, America has been "reforming" its elementary and secondary schools. We've rearranged classrooms and curricula, and coerced staff and students to perform. Still, every month there's another media story documenting how the Japanese, Finns or Germans are knocking us upside the head, and detailing how American kids are stuck near the bottom of the academic heap.

There's finally some good news to report. Even better, it's "news we can use" to improve our schools. The nonprofit RAND research organization has found that the educational reforms of the 1980s and 1990s are demonstrably bearing fruit.

According to RAND's study, titled *Improving Student Achievement: What NAEP Test Scores Tell Us*, math scores nationally are rising one percentile point each year—a pace that adds up quickly. When the study compared states, Texas led the procession, with twice the average gain. Iowa finished in a high-scoring cluster just behind the Lone Star State. California finished dead last in the improvement parade.

The demographic differences between Iowa and California are easy to detect, but Texas and California have almost identical multicultural populations. So why is Texas scoring 11 percentile points higher than California on NAEP math and reading tests?

According to the study, there are three things Texas is doing well that California is not—reducing pupil–teacher ratios in lower grades, funding more public pre-kindergarten programs, and supplying teachers with the resources needed for teaching.

While RAND found that teacher turnover had a statistically significant impact on learning, having "teachers with master's degrees and extensive teaching experience appears to have comparatively little effect on student achievement." Higher salaries also showed little effect, "possibly reflecting the inefficiency of the current compensation system in which pay raises reward both high- and low-quality teachers."

The study suggests salary differences for teachers had little effect across states, but "may have more important achievement effects within states." In other words, higher salaries won't attract a great teacher to Washington Township from Washington, D.C., but might make a difference if the choice is between Washington Township and Washington, Iowa.

What does the 44-state study mean for Mid-Prairie? While we have used state and federal funds to reduce student-teacher ratios in our lower grades (which resulted in big bumps in our test scores), we not only don't have "widespread pre-kindergarten," we don't even have all-day everyday kindergarten—one of just two districts in our 28-school region to share this dubious distinction. It's time for that to change.

Because of recent budget cuts, it's also clear there was some grumbling from the teaching staff about the adequacy of our classroom resources. The RAND study suggests that not only do adequate resources matter to teachers, they matter even more to students.

"Our results certainly challenge the traditional view of public education as 'unreformable,'" RAND concludes, but adds achievement "is still substantially affected by inadequate resources."

Throwing money at problems never solved much, but Republicans and Democrats both agree that the RAND results are worth studying. George W. Bush partisans suggest what Bush did for education in Texas, he can do for the rest of the country. Al Gore supporters argue that the improvements in Texas reflect reforms put in place before Bush became governor, but they still embrace the overall strategies the study suggests.

In the local political arena, the Mid-Prairie Community School District's hard work is also starting to pay off, but it is truly a community effort—and there's more work to be done. Last year we had more small classes in the lower grades, this year we hope to restore more learning resources to our classrooms, and next year we're going to push hard for all-day everyday kindergarten.

With your help, we can make the needle move.

OUGHT TO COMPLAIN ABOUT WORKSHEETS

As this is being written—and perhaps as it's being read—the verdict is out on the presidential election. The media called Florida wrong twice, and the entire election wrong at least once. After the dust settles, we may never know who "really" won.

In some ways, the multiple outcomes resemble those of two prominent education studies by the nonprofit RAND Corporation. This summer, RAND proclaimed Texas to be home of the most-improved schools in the country, particularly for minority students.

Republicans said the study proved the value of George W. Bush's education reforms. Democrats commended the reforms, but claimed they began before Bush became governor.

Then, just before the election, a second RAND report asserted Texas's scores were actually nothing special, and that the previous "improvement" actually reflected weaknesses in its homegrown testing program. As you'd expect, Republicans defended Texas's reforms, while Democrats declared the Lone Star State's "Education Miracle" to be nothing more than a mirage.

Who's right? Your guess is as good as mine—and apparently as good as RAND's. The reason this discussion matters is that the same arguments are being bandied across our state, and within our district.

Iowa, the only state without statewide educational standards, still has definite ideas about what should be measured and how to do it. Iowa requires, among other indicators, regular administrations of the *Iowa Test of Basic Skills* and the *Iowa Tests of Educational Development*. While certain scores are not mandated, it's clear the state considers testing to be an important component of our educational process.

That's not a unanimous opinion. At this fall's board retreat, the value of standardized tests was called into question. A book by Alfie Kohn, perhaps testing's best-known critic, was passed around.

I read several of Kohn's articles. In *Confusing Harder with Better*, Kohn argues that as a result of standardized tests, "The intellectual life is being squeezed out of classrooms, schools are being turned into giant test-prep centers, and many students—as well as some of our finest educators—are being forced out." He adds "high scores are often a sign of lowered standards—a paradox rarely appreciated by those who make, or report on, educational policy."

To a certain extent, Kohn makes sense. It's logical to think time spent on test preparation might result in higher scores—and since time is a limited commodity, that leaves less time for "real learning." However, if you consider that tests such as the *ITBS* and *ITED* attempt to measure mastery of the curriculum, "teaching to the test" actually means "teaching to the curriculum"—which hardly seems a bad thing. If the *ITBS* measures mastery of long division and spelling, for example, I'm not sure what the harm is in teaching those skills to students.

To me, the paradox can be found in a recent Educational Testing Service (ETS) study funded by the Milken Family Foundation, titled *How Teaching Matters: Bringing the Classroom Back Into Discussions of Teacher Quality*. It determined that schools scoring highest on standardized tests spent the most time on hands-on learning and developing higher-order thinking skills—and the least time slogging through the mind-numbing drills Kohn warns about.

Specifically, "In math, students whose teachers emphasize higher-order thinking skills outperform their peers by about 40 percent of a grade level. Students whose teachers conduct hands-on learning outperform their peers by more than 70 percent of a grade level in math and 40 percent of a grade level in science."

Where is the truth? I think it's a lot easier to divine the secret to good teaching than the "truth" regarding the election and the two RAND reports. As evidence, ask yourself who wrote the following statement—the test-hating Kohn, or the test-loving ETS: "Some parents indignantly complain that their kids are bored and can complete the worksheets without break-ing a sweat. They ought to be complaining about the fact that the teacher is relying on worksheets at all."

Kohn? ETS? In this case, Alfie takes the honors, but in truth, both could have claimed authorship. No matter what our political or pedagogical predilections, I hope we would all agree upon the common-sense conclu-sion that the best test prep is outstanding teachers leading enthusiastic students on a learning adventure through a sound curriculum.

If we can reach consensus on this point, we could all claim victory.

GROWING UP THROUGH HISTORY

Any adult who interacts with children is often frustrated by the experi-ence. Kids don't look like us, don't act like us, and most infuriating, don't think like us.

There's now a name for that exasperation. It's called "adultism."

"Just what we need," I thought when I first saw the word. "Another 'ism' to add to racism, sexism and all the other 'isms' on our long list of human failings."

Then I read the definition. "Adultism" refers to our expectations that children demonstrate knowledge and wisdom they have not had time to develop. In short, we want children to be just like us, although it took us decades to reach our present "maturity."

Think of the events outside our children's realm of experience. These high school graduates were born about 1984, after we invaded Grenada. For them, the Vietnam War is probably shelved in the same mental cub-byhole as the Korean War, World War II and, for that matter, the Pelo-ponnesian War.

In technological terms, 2002 grads were born after the CD replaced the LP, which had earlier supplanted the 45 and 78 (yes, youngsters, I'm speaking gibberish). In terms of the arts, they were born seven years AFTER *Star Wars*. Ouch.

When you think about the blank slates that are our children's brains (and I mean that in the nicest possible way), it's obvious we are obliged to bring our kids up to speed. The way to do that, of course, is through our schools.

Lynne Cheney, the wife of our vice president, is a noted public figure herself. A senior fellow at the American Enterprise Institute, she has long advocated teaching history. She observes that in a 1999 survey of Ivy League students, only 20 percent knew that the phrase, "government of the people, by the people, for the people," came from Abraham Lincoln's *Gettysburg Address*.

"We haven't done a good job of teaching our history," Cheney says. "We haven't given young people the knowledge they need to appreciate how greatly fortunate we are to live in freedom."

Cheney, not quite a child of the sixties, nonetheless recommends history "teach-ins" in college classrooms and local libraries. To that list, I'd add our schools—and, I'm pleased to report, the job's being done at Mid-Prairie Middle School.

My son Patrick is in 6th grade. When I visited his social studies room during parent-teacher conferences, I saw that his teacher, Jay Bickford, had adorned his walls with photographs of historical figures—not of presidents, but of kids Patrick's age.

One photo, from 1911, is titled *A Life of Misery; A Young Boy in the Coal Mines*. Its caption tells of Pennsylvania children who labored "six days a week, picking up stones out of coal. Deprived of sunlight and fresh air, they risked being crushed by heavy equipment and mine collapses, being run over by coal cars, being deprived of limbs by axes and falling debris, and developing lung diseases by inhaling toxic particles."

Other photos show children working in infectious bean canneries, poisonous paint factories, and even as pin setters in bowling alleys, where they "breathed in tobacco smoke and often smoked themselves, were offered drinks, heard lewd stories and witnessed violence."

Who was president of the United States in 1911? Whoever he was, he probably wasn't as important as the kids on Mr. Bickford's wall in terms of shaping my view of the world.

As part of Patrick's education, I hope he also learns not every child in history had it as good as he and his friends do, and that the same can be said of most children today.

While her husband is sometimes considered our nation's "ultimate adult," Lynne Cheney is right on target when she insists we teach our children that "Freedom is not our inevitable heritage. . . . Were we to lose it, liberty might not come our way again."

Two footnotes: First, the president in 1911 was . . . William Howard Taft (but you knew that, right?). Second, Patrick complained mightily about the writing cramps he developed during the hour he laboriously hand-copied Mr. Bickford's captions in service to this column.

At the risk of sounding "adultist," it seems my kid has some growing up to do.

Chapter Six

Community

ENGLISH AND THEN SOME!

There's a relentless effort in the Iowa Legislature to pass an *English Only* bill, and this year it might have the votes to become law. Supporters say *English Only* promotes state unity, and saves our government the cost of conducting business in multiple languages. They profess that their interest in uniformity lies solely in their reverence for community cohesion and good government.

As a school board member, it is in my economic interest to take our leaders at their word—but as a board member, I am also responsible to the educational values I have sworn to uphold. In that second role, I can't help but wonder about the wisdom of a policy that aims to proclaim, "If you come to Iowa, you better speak English because we don't know anything else—and we like it that way."

Consider our last century. Two-thirds of Iowa's counties lost population during the 1900s, a reality that is crippling local tax bases and school districts. More than anything else, most towns today just need people. Posting signs at our borders declaring *Welcome, Newcomers! (As Long As You're Just Like Us!)* hardly seems likely to reverse our literal demographic death spiral.

As the member of a household jointly headed by a Taiwanese immigrant, I can tell you for a fact that in considering hypothetical moves to two states—one that warns outsiders that *English Only* need apply, and another that quietly recognizes that social pressures will erase most differences in a generation or less—that the *Come As You Are* state would be much more likely to attract us, our kids, our talents and our tax dollars.

If our leaders want Iowa to fare better this century than in the past one, instead of pushing outsiders to conform to our ways, we should strive to become more fluent in the ways of the world—and have our schools lead the charge. Instead of embracing our linguistic limitations, we should make it clear that Iowa is an open-minded state that values all people and cultures.

That doesn't mean *English Only*. That translates into *English and Then Some!*

Today, most districts start seriously teaching foreign languages in high school, after the brains in question have lost the plasticity needed to easily pick up a second tongue. If we started teaching new languages in kindergarten and kept at it for 13 years, our graduates would not only be multilingual, but would have better understandings of the rules of all language—including English.

It doesn't matter which language you pick—as long as it's not *English Only*. During my own education, I found no topic more tedious than dividing subjects from predicates in English language sentences. Despite making my living with words, I've also found no skill more useless. Still, that's the kind of English we too often teach our kids.

If I were Iowa's education czar (oops, non-English word!), I'd decree that our smallest students be taught anything but the musty rules of English syntax. Instead, by studying a second language, kids would actually discover why grammar is important, and come to terms early with the apparently unfortunate reality that not all people speak, act or even think the way "we" do.

As a registered Republican, it's within my rights to observe that we "conservatives" are among the strongest supporters of *English Only* legislation, but exactly what is it that we're "conserving"? Most families didn't arrive in America speaking the King's English—in the local neighborhood, we often spoke German, Czech, Welsh and, in the case of my kids, Chinese.

True conservatives would recognize the tragedy of failing to conserve our linguistic legacies, instead of insisting that the rest of the world be "dumbed down" (to use an educational term) to our unexceptional standards.

This column may make some people angry. Good.

To use the vernacular, it's time for Iowans to realize the world doesn't revolve around our pale white posteriors. If we can't get that message through to our leaders, what chance do we have with our children, or for our Iowa's future?

STARS OF THE WEEK

"Remarkable" home, school and community partnerships don't just happen. They're the products of hard work, open doors, smiling faces and inviting institutions.

Last Tuesday, two dozen teachers, parents and administrators gathered in a formal effort to forge such relationships in an event titled *Remarkable Home/School Partnership*. The participants analyzed where Kalona Elementary excelled in terms of communicating with its constituencies, and then collectively brainstormed a vision for the future. While each of several subgroups had its own impressions and ideas, most also reached a common set of conclusions.

High marks went out to teacher newsletters, fliers and *Friday Folders* designed to keep parents in the loop on the accomplishments, challenges and events taking place in their kids' classrooms. As a parent of two students, I can testify that each of my kids' teachers puts out a great product.

Mrs. Juilfs, Patrick's 4th-grade teacher, has weekly fliers chock-full of information about her students' noteworthy achievements, challenges the class might be encountering with certain subjects, and events to look forward to in the weeks to come. While it's virtually impossible for me, much less for 20-plus other parents, to speak with any teacher once each week, because of Mrs. Juilfs's weekly update, I always feel I know what's going on.

Mrs. Bell, Molly's 2nd-grade teacher, has a different style that is no less effective. As a faithful reader of her bi-weekly publication, I can tell you a little bit about each of her students through her *Star of the Week* student profile, what units the students have completed, and what the class has to look forward to in its curriculum.

Other KES successes include the contributions of Booster Club members and other volunteers in holding events that not only raise literally thousands of dollars to support our schools, but also help create an educational environment in which learning can flourish.

While a lot is going right, the participants thought we could do even better—which is as it should be. Among the ideas brought forward were "room buddies" who could provide parents new to the school a helping hand in becoming fully integrated into the school community.

While paper-based newsletters are wonderful, many participants looked forward to more use of e-mail and classroom web pages through which questions could be addressed, reminders could be sent, and achievements celebrated. Electronic communications were seen as rapid, reliable (they don't get lost on the way home) and convenient means of keeping in touch.

From my perspective, I was most interested in suggestions for making it easier to get community members involved with our schools. While two dozen people made it to the meeting, there were reportedly others prevented from doing so by child-care concerns. The participants suggested that if we want parental involvement, we need to keep in mind parental responsibilities as well.

Other discussions focused on developing creative ways to bridge the town-gown divide. Ideas included bringing in grandparents as volunteers and book readers, and having businesses adopt classrooms. One great suggestion was holding presentations on our schools during community-oriented events. Earlier this month, hundreds of people attended the Kalona Fun Night. I'd bet that many parents might have welcomed the chance to hear a 20-minute presentation on what's going on in the schools from the teachers, school board or administration.

The bottom line is that once people have visited our schools and gotten to know our students on a personal level, it's much easier to understand what our educational issues are, how they're being addressed and, most important, what's at stake.

I hope it was the first of many "Remarkable" evenings to come.

REACH FOR THE STARS

Imagine yourself standing on a chair, reaching high to pull down a letter-sized piece of paper taped to a wall. The paper has a business's name on it, and next to it, there's another paper with another name, and next to it, another—as far as you can see.

By the time you work your way around the 200-foot perimeter of the room, with each foot home to another mini-poster, you can't help but say to yourself, "Man, that's a lot of paper!"

That was exactly my position after the recent Kalona Elementary School Fun Night. Literally hundreds of community supporters had reached deep to underwrite the evening's events through contributions of goods, services and cash—earning themselves small posters in the process. Their donations, combined with hundreds of hours of volunteer labor, enabled kids to enjoy a wholesome evening's entertainment, and raise several thousand dollars for the KES Booster Club in the process.

The success of Fun Night proves beyond a doubt Mid-Prairie cares about its kids. A quick glance through the current newspaper finds 12 column inches' worth of donors to the M-P Music Boosters, and notice of substantial Lions Club, Volunteer Ambulance and Knights of Columbus scholarships.

Turn another page and you'll find four students with perfect papers winning weekly prizes from the telephone cooperative, and last—but certainly not least—there's news that the athletic boosters have raised $154,000 toward the new weight room.

Sadly, Mid-Prairie's staunch supporters have few nationwide peers. According to *Action for All*, a new study commissioned by the Public Education Network and *Education Week* magazine, 91 percent of Americans consider education to be "every child's birthright," but only 22 percent say "people in their community 'take a lot of' responsibility for insuring quality public schools."

Of the 1,175 surveyed, the study found many "want to help, but only in limited ways and often motivated by a life-or-death crisis, such as a school shooting or a state takeover. . . . Problems of overcrowding in schools, chronically low test scores, and young people not getting jobs would not motivate a majority of Americans to take action."

The excuses for inaction are disappointing. Nearly 70 percent claim to have "zero to three hours a week to help improve the quality of education" (even though other studies find TVs turned on twice that long EACH DAY in most homes).

Most also argue they "lack crucial information and expertise" needed to help. My guess is most 1st graders would think anyone able to read to them already knows plenty.

The respondents readily admit wanting "quick and easy" ways to help our schools, such as voting, signing petitions, or talking up schools with their neighbors (although fewer than 10 percent actually vote in school board elections).

Acknowledging this imperfect starting point, the authors suggest *Ten Things You Can Do Today* to improve our schools. Idea One is seeking out information on education issues. The respondents most trusted teachers to provide good information, but had less faith in school board members and newspapers (which says a lot for this column).

Other ideas include seeking out student achievement data, attending school board meetings (most are under three hours), talking to parents, and visiting local schools.

While any community can always do better, it's clear Mid-Prairie leads the pack when it comes to investing sweat equity. While I pulled down posters, a team of parents counted thousands of 25-cent tickets for more than an hour. Other boosters worked still later to put chairs back in place, vacuum floors, tear down booths and pack up equipment—which they would then come back to pick up the next day.

These volunteers, and the many others like them throughout our district, didn't have any more spare hours than most of those participating in the *Action for All* survey, but found them anyway. The community should be proud of itself, and of its students, for inspiring that uncommon level of commitment.

RENAISSANCE OF COMMUNITY SUPPORT

This week, scores of Mid-Prairie High School students walked across the stage before beaming family and friends to pick up well-earned certificates documenting their achievements. It's still several months early for graduation, but the citations being distributed symbolized real achievement—not only by our students, but by our community as a whole.

The *Renaissance Awards* are tangible tokens of accomplishment presented to Mid-Prairie students who had perfect attendance records, earned spots on the honor roll, or demonstrated significant improvements in their grade point averages or work habits. For their hard work, the students received gift certificates from businesses ranging from Best Buy to Billups Construction, and from Paul Revere's Pizza to Precision Structures.

While learning is its own reward, it doesn't hurt our kids— or community—to encourage the ongoing investments of effort required to achieve academic excellence. When the *Renaissance Awards* program was first announced, the students themselves were its toughest critics. They wondered aloud why they were having to come back to the high school at night for another assembly, and as the program began, they reportedly used their math skills to calculate just how soon they'd be able to leave.

Then, a funny thing happened. Instead of being bored out of their minds, those minds began to grasp what was happening. Kids from all rungs of the academic ladder, from future valedictorians to back-of-the-packers who still put forth real effort each day, were being rewarded for doing things right. Moreover, whether they had picked up an academic letter for their jackets, or coupons for compact disks, their strolls across the stage weren't complete until they had posed for the local newspapers — which resulted in yet another chance to show off their achievements before the community.

If you were to judge our society not by reading newspapers but by watching television, it would sometimes seem that what counts in life is the car you drive, or whether you consistently connect with your jump shot. In contrast, the moral of the *Renaissance Awards* is that unglamorous endeavors like showing up for class, getting your homework done, and making the most of your abilities deserve equal accolades.

What makes the *Renaissance Awards* successful is not only the hard work of our students, but the far-sighted support of our local businesses, five of which offered $750 or more in support. As businesspeople, they don't invest hard-earned dollars without expecting commensurate returns. After running the numbers, they concluded their best returns would be realized investing in hard-working high school students.

The first lesson in *Education 101* is that positive reinforcement works. The *Renaissance Awards* celebration is evidence that as a community, we have learned well.

GREAT PR IS IN THE BAG

Just before Thanksgiving, I had a delightful surprise. Like the other lucky local shoppers who responded "Paper" to the question "Paper or Plastic?," I didn't just receive a bulky bag in which to stuff my groceries, but a brown paper canvas upon which a kindergartner had produced an original work of art.

The illustrations were in honor of *American Education Week,* but are emblematic of the year-round efforts successful districts use to cement relationships with their schools. Shortly before my shopping surprise, I attended the Iowa Association of School Boards convention. One session, titled *Building Community Understanding of School Achievement,* offered an arm-long list of initiatives to help schools to bridge the "Town/Gown" gap. The following are just a handful of the excellent ideas:

Universal Minutes. In one district, a participant at each school meeting—whether of the board, PTA or boosters—provides official meeting minutes to the central office. The district makes copies for notebooks available in each of its 20 buildings. Any parent, citizen or employee can go anywhere in the district to find out what's going on. Good information abounds, enabling folks to act upon initiatives rather than on unfounded rumors.

Readable Reports. All districts are required to submit annual reports to the Iowa Department of Education. Most often, the reports are thick with hard-to-digest data and contain text only a bureaucrat could love. One district makes a conscious effort to transform its data into easy-on-the-eye documents everyone can understand. Not surprisingly, the district has discovered the more people know about their schools, the more likely they are to support them.

Art Everywhere. This district bragged about hanging student art in its boardroom for all the world to see. While a good step, personally I'm more impressed by our paper bags. I'd also love to see rotating art displays in highly public places—for example, banks, libraries and post offices.

Program Reviews. While a different sort of "PR," this district determined that for its taxpayers to be confident their dollars were being well spent, it needed to review each of its educational programs every three years—no exceptions—and fix or eliminate those sapping strength from the district. Regular program reviews not only made a difference in dollars, they found, but also in terms of the public's perception of their overall educational efforts.

Show and Tell. It's sometimes difficult to differentiate school board meetings from those of a city council. The meetings I remember most during my time on the board are those involving students. We've had inventors and musicians share their talents with us in the past. Bringing kids to board meetings, or to civic organizations ranging from the Rotarians to senior citizens, is something that can't happen too often.

Boys (and Girls) on the Bus. Students visiting senior citizens is great, but senior citizens visiting students may be even better. In this community, school buses picked up scores of seniors for four-hour tours of the schools. By sitting in on classes, listening to performances, and even sharing school lunches, the residents had much more understanding and enthusiasm for the schools they may have last entered a generation or two before.

Great public relations are not just "spin." It's telling people what's been accomplished and what remains to be done. If people trust you, they'll listen to what you have to say, even when you're asking for their time, hard work or money. They may not always agree with you, but they'll usually hear you out, which is all we can ask.

As educators, we must remember most community members will never step inside our classrooms. Since we can't always bring the public to our schools, we have to be creative in bringing our schools to the public—and that's why I'm so partial to the recent paper-bag productions of our smallest scholars.

Everyone who received a hand-crayoned grocery bag during American Education Week thought about our schools and smiled. PR doesn't get any better than that.

PUT YOUR FINGERPRINTS ON SOME BLUEPRINTS

After two years, the good editors who publish the *Report Card* and I have our routine down to a science. I send in 700 words via e-mail, they reformat the file to fit their conventions, move the text over to the page, and we're done.

I don't ask second chances to send submissions because once it's done, it's done—and I'm sure they want it to stay that way. Besides, there's always next week.

Next Monday, citizens from across Mid-Prairie will also be working on a semiliterary endeavor, the new Kalona Library, but in this case, there is "no next week." A new library comes to a community perhaps once a century, which is why it's so important that you drop in to the "charrette" [final, intense effort to meet a deadline] being held at the Chamber of Commerce.

Already, Mid-Prairie students are making arrangements to tell the architects what kids look for in a library. If mine are any indication, they might like internally lighted "blocks" into which they could crawl and semi-uncomfortably read books. The blocks would be just right for getting "alone" with a work of literature, but still maintaining visual contact with parents or teachers. They would also be small enough that grown-ups couldn't fit inside them, which would make them all the more cool—kind of on-the-ground tree houses for which small size, for once, is an advantage.

My tree house days are probably over, but I would still love a reading lounge illuminated by natural light. You can't bring the library outdoors, but you can bring the outdoors into the library.

Based upon your informational and architectural interests, you may also have a wish list for the library. The charrette is your chance—probably even your great-great-great grandchildren's chance—to put some fingerprints on a local library's design.

You don't need to stay the whole six hours. You just need to drop in, see what's going on, and share your ideas. Remember, though, when the architects are done, they won't return in your lifetime. Make sure you don't miss your chance.

LAZY DAYS OF SUMMER

After more than a month of downtime, Mid-Prairie students are deep into the grooves of their summer vacations. Tans are in place, swimming skills are down pat, and any kid worth his or her salt has by now mastered the fine art of not doing much at all.

Not to be a spoilsport, but they better enjoy it while they can. A growing body of research suggests students who slack off DURING the school year pay the price in academic performance. A Rochester, New York, study found that students scoring in the top sixth of their classes on standardized tests attended school 93 percent of the time. Students in the next highest group attended at a 91 percent rate, while the bottom half made it to class at only an 85 percent clip.

According to *USA Today*, "The notion that students with the best attendance perform better is so simple, so obvious, that it may elicit a 'well, duh' from parents and educators."

But if it is so obvious, what are we—as parents and educators—doing to encourage simply showing up? While my memory may be fading, my recollection of the 1960s-era Hussey attendance policy is, "Unless a bone is sticking out, I don't want to hear about it." I don't know that any of us earned perfect attendance awards, but except for the years we got chicken pox, I'll bet we never missed more than one day a month—a rough translation of Rochester's highest attendance rate.

Parental commitment can make itself apparent in more ways than one, sometimes in spectacular fashion. This June, George Abraham Thampy (remember the name—you may be hearing it again when he wins the Nobel Prize) won the National Spelling Bee, which carried a $10,000 cash prize, along with a $1,000 Savings Bond and an encyclopedia. The 12-year-old's winning word was *demarche.*

That's impressive enough, but it was all in a week's work for Thampy, who a few days earlier had placed second in the National Geography Bee. He fell short when he came up with "only" one of the three major geographic regions of Denmark.

"My mom and dad taught me everything," says Thampy, who like the second- and third-place finishers in the Spelling Bee is home-schooled. His parents are from India, and have made education—his and theirs—a family priority. According to his mother, Bina, while she was teaching him spelling, George was teaching her English. "He would gently tell me, 'Mom, I don't think that's the right pronunciation.'"

This month at the British Open, another outstanding parent has a good chance of watching his son, Tiger Woods, wrap a ribbon around his claim of being the best golfer the world has ever known—at the age of 24. Earl Woods taught Tiger to love, respect and devote countless hours to the sport he has come to dominate. They now share their joint passion with inner city children through the Tiger Woods Foundation.

"People have no idea how many hours I put into this game," said Tiger in *Sports Illustrated.* "My dad always told me, 'There are no short cuts.' These kids may not play golf. They may not be what I am in a golfing sense. But they could be what I am in a business field or a medical field."

"What we want to do is improve these kids' chances in life," said Earl. "They learn how to handle success, failure, integrity and patience."

We may be in the lazy days of summer, but it may be time to start thinking about doing in Kalona and Wellman what they've already done in

Rochester, where the Business Alliance is encouraging local employers—including Xerox and Kodak—to check the attendance rates of students applying for jobs at their companies.

"For many of us, this is intuitive," says Virginia Cornyn of Xerox, speaking for the Alliance. "But now that we've got the data backing it up, we can go out and beat the drum."

BOOM! BOOM! BOOM! This week, that's the sound of fireworks going off, but come late August, let's hope it's the sound of a drumbeat around the district, where Lesson One will be "If you want to get ahead of the crowd, get your behind to class."

ENTHUSIASTICALLY EMBRACING SELF-STUDY

In 1992, my employer—Prince William Sound Community College in Valdez, Alaska—was spinning out of control. Two years earlier, our founding president had taken a leave of absence to run for Congress. An interim president filled in, the founding president lost his race and returned to PWSCC for a year, and then left a second time—this time for good—to make another run at the job.

Stepping in as our second interim president was Dr. James Bemis, the retired Executive Director of the Commission on Colleges of the Northwest Association of Schools and Colleges. That's a huge title, but it reflected his 25-year tenure as the head of the college-accrediting agency for the seven northwestern United States.

PWSCC's accreditation renewal—allows schools and their students to receive state and federal funds—was coming up in 1994, at which point we would have had five presidents in four years. Some wondered whether we should ask for a delay until we had a "permanent" president to lead us.

Dr. Bemis told us what he tells everyone. It's during transitions that it's most important schools determine what they believe in and where they stand. With Dr. Bemis guiding us, we jumped in with both feet, and emerged two years later with a new president and one of the more glowing self-study evaluations issued by the Commission.

Mid-Prairie is not in the same boat as PWSCC, but we are in a time of transition. We are hiring a superintendent, the state has recently begun demanding annual Comprehensive School Improvement Plan (CSIP) reports from each district, and our North Central Association review is looming. As Jim Bemis might say, we could offer no better gift to our new superintendent than a running start on a districtwide analysis of where we're at, where we want to be and how we intend to get there.

At our first February board meeting, Mid-Prairie administrators will present student achievement data. Following their report, I've asked for us to begin creating the district-level committees necessary to conduct an exemplary self-study.

I know less than many about Iowa's school improvement process, but I also know what's necessary for these analyses to result in profound cultural changes—I've lived it.

First, you designate a steering committee to drive the effort.

Second, that team explains self-study purposes and procedures to literally every interested party—including staff, students, governing boards and the public.

Third, every employee is assigned to a subcommittee, and is required to contribute in some measure. The subcommittees focus on "standards" such as curriculum, the physical plant and administrative control.

Fourth, the steering committee helps the subcommittees develop research instruments, coordinate surveys, and review the resulting data and analyses. A consolidated report is drafted, and at our college, every employee was required to read the entire document and sign a statement to that effect—and to their credit, absolutely everyone actually did both.

Fifth, you host evaluators. Our visitors' most striking observation was that every staff member, most students, and even a local resident at the airport luggage carousel knew the team was coming and how important our self-study was to our college.

Sixth, you use the wisdom gained to improve your school on an ongoing basis. If that doesn't happen, all you've accomplished is wasting time and killing trees.

I've already heard it said that the various demands for data are keeping folks from doing their "real jobs." I'd counter that a first-class self-study gives every person who cares about our schools the insight and information necessary to help achieve our common aspirations, which makes our employees' "real jobs" that much easier to accomplish.

Iowa, alone among the 50 states, does not have mandated standards for student achievement, believing those are best determined locally. That unique privilege brings with it an extra measure of responsibility. Unless we want someone else telling us what our standards are, we must embrace every opportunity to work them out for ourselves.

MAILBOXES, MAYHEM—AND MAYBE PROGRESS?

Like many of you, I recently spent more time than I wanted to with my right arm extended, my head turned toward the ground, and my face twisted into a grimace, doing what was once a delightfully dull task— opening the mailbox.

The mailbox bomber missed Mid-Prairie by a few miles, but it was too close for comfort. During the four days he terrorized middle America, the same warped mentality was at work around the world: a suicide bombing in Israel derailed a meeting of George W. Bush and Ariel Sharon; a murderer silenced Pim Fortuyn, a flamboyant Netherlands politician; and French voters gave far-right Jean-Marie Le Pen an unsettling measure of electoral approval.

Whether in Iowa or Israel, those who use mayhem to "send a message" seem to share two traits: they believe they've received the short end of some sociopolitical stick, and consider themselves so inarticulate that they must use violence to do their talking.

In other words, they need healthy doses of what honest educations can provide—an understanding of individuals and organizations beyond their direct experience, and the ability to voice—through words—any residual concerns over perceived oppressions.

Education is not a panacea against sociopaths—but for the potentially disaffected, it might be the best place to start. In France, Le Pen was supported by what *Business Week* called the "have-nots: the unemployed, lower-income workers, and people under 25, many of whom are jobless or have temporary work."

In addition to providing tools to share in our future, education also gives us the chance to explore our past, the lessons from which many in France seemed to have forgotten. According to MSNBC, Le Pen proposed "illegal aliens be placed in 'transit camps' before deportation and that a 'special train' be organized to send them to Britain—chilling Nazi-era language."

I had the good fortune to be born after World War II, and attained adulthood after America's biggest civil rights battles were fought and generally won. Still, it was just seven years ago that I visited a Montana tribal college and was told matter-of-factly by a Crow student that the public school he attended was "integrated," but it was also understood white kids sat on one side of the aisle and Indian kids on the other.

That same year his high school alma mater tried to hold a conference celebrating cultural diversity. It was a disaster. According to the Montana Human Rights Network, "Rather than having a celebratory flavor, the conference highlighted the town's racial divisions. Nearly 200 . . . students—150 of whom had NOTES FROM THEIR PARENTS (my emphasis)—did not attend the conference. Three days later, hate literature from the Ku Klux Klan and the Church of the Creator was distributed in the community."

Fortunately, progress is being made. Just before the last alleged conspirator went on trial for a 39-year-old church bombing that killed four girls in Birmingham, Alabama, high school seniors in Butler, Georgia held its first integrated prom—at the students' insistence.

According to the *Christian Science Monitor*, locals conceded "some resistance to the idea of a mixed prom," particularly among the older generation. Said the friend of one man the paper attempted to interview, "Don't get him started. I've got to work with him the rest of the afternoon."

Nonetheless, the 200 seniors held sway—at least those who supported the change. The class vote was 2-to-1 for integration, which implies a third of this year's Butler seniors voted for continued segregation (a higher proportion than the French who voted for Le Pen).

Next year, Mid-Prairie plans to ramp up its celebration of Martin Luther King's birthday, honoring a man who lost his life in service to nonviolent political change. It's not the entire solution, but it's a start.

Education may never stop zealots willing to destroy others or themselves, but if we take its lessons to heart—valuing searching over certainty, acceptance over adherence, and freedom over fear—we may slow some down.

In a world in which we now wince while opening the mailbox, that's progress.

SLEEPING THROUGH A REVOLUTION

When my grandparents were born, in the early 1900s, lynchings were not uncommon events, occurring as far north as Duluth, Minn. When my parents were born in the 1930s, segregation was the law of the land, by code down south and by custom most other places.

When I was born, in 1960, there was no Civil Rights Act, no Voting Rights Act, and Alabama's George Wallace had yet to roar "Segregation now! Segregation tomorrow! Segregation forever!" It wasn't until 1978, the year I graduated from high school, that the last students who started 1st grade in some "separate-but-equal" Louisiana schools also received their hard-earned diplomas.

Now that we're in a shiny new century, it's me who's the relic of history. Still, the battle for racial justice is far from over—and education is taking center stage in the struggle.

This year as we celebrated Martin Luther King's birthday, President Bush said, "Education is the great civil rights issue of our time. . . . Dr. Martin Luther King Jr. would accept no less than an equal concern for every child in America, and neither will my administration."

By birth and politics, Bush may represent the privileged class, but his words are in harmony with voices across the racial spectrum. Harvard's Henry Louis Gates, in a PBS interview with Jesse Jackson, said, "When I was growing up, the blackest thing you could be in our community was Thurgood Marshall or Dr. King. But I recently read the results of a Gallup poll of inner city black children in Washington that asked them to list 'things white.' And on that list were: getting straight As, speaking standard English—even going to the Smithsonian Institute."

Jackson responded that our media teach black kids to revere less desirable role models by portraying African Americans "as less intelligent than we are, less hard-working than we work . . . and less worthy than we are. . . . There's a competition for the minds of our children. You teach four, five, ten, twelve, twenty students. And mass media is teaching by the tens of thousands."

The terrible job our society does in teaching blacks and whites about race doesn't just affect big cities and the states where the people talk funny. The unfortunate truth is that as you read this, Iowa has the highest rate of African American incarceration in the United States. My guess is that part of the problem is that we look around at the few black faces we see, avoid saying or doing hateful things, and think we've got the problem licked.

Judging by our dismal record, simply demonstrating good manners ain't good enough. As we move into Black History Month, perhaps we should take to heart King's speech, *Remaining Awake Through a Great Revolution*, which he delivered in Grinnell, Iowa, among other places, in 1967.

> Anyone who feels that we can live without being concerned about other individuals and other nations is sleeping through a revolution. . . .
>
> It may well be that we will have to repent in this generation, not merely for the vitriolic works and violent actions of the bad people who bomb a church in Birmingham, Alabama, or shoot down a civil rights worker in Selma, but for the appalling silence and indifference of the good people who sit around and say, "Wait on time."
>
> Human progress never rolls in on wheels of inevitability. It comes through the tireless efforts and the persistent work of dedicated individuals. Without this hard work, time becomes an ally of the primitive forces of social stagnation. So we must help time and realize that the time is always right to do right. . . .
>
> Never allow it to be said that you are silent onlookers, detached spectators, but that you are involved participants in the struggle to make justice a reality.

This may be Black History Month, but as Dr. King maintained, there's never a wrong time to share with students the lessons of your lives and your hopes for their futures.

Don't "wait on time." Do it now, in a classroom or across the kitchen table. As someone old enough to have experienced black history, white history and human history, there is no better person to teach history's lessons than you.

Chapter Seven

Dollars

TO THE SPOILED GOES THE WINNING?

The recently completed Drake Relays are arguably Iowa's purest test of athletic ability. In contrast to figure skating, or even football, where opinions often decide outcomes, track-and-field is meritocratic. If you run the fastest, you win—and can rightfully claim to be the best.

Or can you? If a kid grows up on potato chips and processed cheese, and his neighbor eats only fruits, vegetables and lean protein, is their race still fair? If one school strong-arms an inexperienced teacher into coaching track, while another recruits an Olympic-caliber decathlete, who's going to win? Anyone care to bet on the rookie?

In our educational system, and our economy, some would also argue the rewards also go to the swift and strong—and to some extent, they're right.

But what about a boy who grows up in a house with no books? What about a girl whose parents can't afford a posh private school's tuition? If those children someday "lose" races for college admissions or fast-track jobs to students who enjoyed those advantages, were the less-prepared kids really any less deserving?

I can't make that argument in good conscience. Nonetheless, the cold hard data suggest we are doing little to make the contest fairer. In fact, the numbers suggest just the opposite.

Using U.S. Census figures, the Iowa Policy Project found that during the 1990s, the richest fifth of Iowans' incomes soared 43 percent to an average of $131,668. The bottom fifth "enjoyed" 3.4 percent increases that nudged their pay to $16,586. Do the math, and you'll find their wages increased less than 3 cents per hour per year—before taxes.

While I applaud the proudly liberal IPP for bringing the disparity to light, I part company with its solutions. Its leaders seem to favor "top-down" remedies such as wage-and-price controls, protectionist trade laws and more generous welfare policies. I worry less about outcomes than inputs— and "inputs" is what schools are all about.

Wages are only as permanent as the next round of layoffs, and can't be sustained if employee output doesn't exceed employer income. Outstanding educations—and the value they provide to both employees and employers— can never be taken away.

That's why, no matter where each of us sits on the political spectrum— left, right or above it all—we should agree to invest what it takes to provide fair shots at success for all America's children. In the words of Harvard's William Julius Wilson, unless we revitalize our "equalizing institutions," America could become a "two-tiered society . . . in which the successful upper- and middle-classes live lives fundamentally different from the working classes and the poor."

Occasionally, those who work in education probably seem like nags— never satisfied with the support for their endeavors, and too quick to lay on guilt trips.

Well, as at the Drake Relays, America's educational and economic systems also have winners and losers, but in these games, the stakes are much higher than the fleeting admiration of friends and family.

Too often, "winning" these races means being positioned for lifelong health and happiness, while "losing" means working hard and dying young. With stakes that high, no one should apologize for aggressively supporting every child's right to a first-rate education.

Even if every child ate healthful foods and enjoyed Olympic-caliber coaching, each event at the Drake Relays would still just have one winner. That's the nature of sports.

However, it is our great fortune that almost any American whose body and brain are well nourished as children stands an excellent chance for success in life.

During the 1990s, our "equalizing institutions" failed to keep pace with other forces in our society. The proof was in the annual 3-cent raises for those whose wages, and lives, were already unequal.

This year in the state capital, our schools stumbled out of the starting blocks and never caught up, attracting less than a 1 percent increase in funding. As we set about educating the next generation, it's time to dust ourselves off and get back in the race.

ALWAYS PLAY AGAINST PAR

Tiger Woods may be tearing up the links of the 21st century, but for many of the past 100 years, Sam Snead had the sweetest swing in golf. The secret to Snead's six decades of success may have been his philosophy, "Forget about your opponents. Always play against par."

Just as golf is a sport about numbers, so is this column, specifically those with dollar signs in front of them. While I don't want to judge ourselves against our statewide peers, sometimes it helps to understand where we're at by handicapping ourselves against par.

Mid-Prairie's property taxes stand at $12.19, compared with $12.91 across Iowa. We're lucky to enjoy relative affluence, with a taxable property valuation per pupil of $213,384, compared with a state average of $185,750. In other words, our citizens enjoy noticeably lower tax rates against appreciably higher property valuations—both good things from a strictly pecuniary perspective.

Mid-Prairie's income taxes are also easy on the average wallet. In 1999, we collected $2,789 per student, $602 less than the state average of $3,391.

Of course, lower taxes paid means less money collected, and there's no financial flimflam that can keep that fiscal reality from affecting our classrooms. Our general fund expenses per pupil for 2000 were $5,874, or $462 less than Iowa's typical $6,336.

Of the $5,874, we spend $3,705 on salaries, $191 less than normal, and $828 on benefits, $124 less than average. At $464, our purchased services are $156 "below par," while at $467, we spend $86 more than most districts on supplies per student.

Our "property" spending per pupil is $114, compared with $159 statewide; "other objects" per pupil are $22, exactly the average; and we have $274 flowing through Mid-Prairie to our area education association, compared with $305 across the state.

Spending less may be good or bad, depending upon your perspective, but we also have less in the bank, which almost no one enjoys. Do the division, and you'll discover Mid-Prairie has $382 in fund balances associated with each student, while Iowa's average is $625.

The other side of the economic equation is what you do with your dollars, and the data suggest our answer is "a lot." Our student/teacher ratio is 13, compared with a state average of 14.4. The typical district maintains 4.1 buildings, but we're teaching in 5.

You run the numbers, and it's clear we're driving a Chevrolet, not a Cadillac—or even a Buick, Tiger's vehicle of choice. That may be OK, since all three models can take you from Point A to Point B (which is also the point of education), but you still need to change the oil every once in a while and thankfully, we're also investing more in that.

This year, local voters approved increasing our Physical Plant and Equipment Levy. That will raise our property tax rates from $12.19 to $12.44—or a quarter per thousand dollars assessed valuation (and still 45 cents less than the statewide average).

Our income tax surtax rate will likely be boosted a point, from 4 to 5—which means we'll be collecting one penny more for every dollar our residents pay in state taxes. If you paid $2,000 in state taxes last year, you'll pay $20 more next year—not nothing, but probably not a crushing burden either.

This column is not about asking for more money. It's simply an attempt to do at a local level what most families do periodically around the kitchen table—figure out what's coming in, what's going out, and what's left over. Knowing those things, we can make better decisions about what we want to do next.

Are we keeping up with the Joneses? Should we care? Sam Snead may have been playing against par, but you can bet he knew where Bobby Jones was on the leader board.

Still, education is less about prevailing over others than it is about improving ourselves. Perhaps the dancer Mikhail Baryshnikov captured it even better than the duffer Snead when he said, "I do not try to dance better than anyone else. I only try to dance better than myself."

Greatness doesn't occur without time, talent and determination, but knowing how much we have budgeted for lessons is as good a first step as any.

IT'S ONLY MONEY

After six months on the board, I've learned that many of the most important issues facing the Mid-Prairie School District receive scant public attention, while some marginal issues have a surprising tendency to attract a crowd. On Monday, there's going to be a $9,426,061 item on our agenda. Unfortunately, I'm told that if history is any guide, our public hearing on next year's budget will play to an empty house.

That's too bad. While looking at numbers add up on a spreadsheet isn't as exciting as seeing them pile up on a scoreboard, our budget makes everything else possible. While I'm far from an accountant, this article represents my best effort to let you know why we spend our money the way we do—in one thousand words or less.

Of our nearly $9.5 million budget, almost $7.9 million is in the Operating Fund. That's the money we use to pay salaries, buy supplies, keep our lights on and our buildings warm. It also includes nearly $400,000 that flows through to the Grant Wood Area Education Agency, and tuition that goes to other school districts (more about that later).

Of the $7.9 million in the Operating Fund, more than $6 million is allocated for employee expenditures. As a board, we would like nothing more than to hire and retain the best possible teaching and support staff. However, when such a large proportion of our spending is earmarked for salaries and benefits, small increases in compensation have huge effects on our budget. For example, a 3 percent across-the-board raise would result in a $184,780 budget increase—or nearly 80 percent of our Undesignated Unspent Balance of $233,243, which is essentially the money we have in the bank.

Theoretically, if your bank balance is printed in black ink, you have enough cash to get by, but the reality is that not having a modest cushion actually costs us money. The Iowa Department of Education recommends that school districts maintain a 5 percent solvency ratio. Given next year's operating budget, that's $394,828.

Because we weren't able to meet that standard last year, we missed an opportunity to refinance our debt. A half percentage point savings would have netted us $20,000 in annual interest savings. Without getting too algebraic, spending $20,000 less on interest is the same as earning 12 percent on a $166,666 investment, the amount that would have brought us to our 5 percent ratio. If you've hung with me this long, the moral of the story is we could have spent the same amount on our students last year and had more money in the bank had we not spent down our surplus in years past. In the long run, our students are better off if we manage our money as prudently as possible.

I'd like to be able to report that through some fiscal sleight-of-hand, we've been able to spare our students from the side effects of our budgetary struggles, but I can't. For example, in 1991, we spent $68,725 on textbooks, and spent $77,031 as recently as 1998. This year, our textbook bill is $16,269. Over the decade, textbooks skyrocketed in cost, while our spending on them crashed and burned. You can't tell me our students haven't suffered as a result.

How do we get out of this fix? While it's always possible to save a nickel here and a dime there, we've pinched most pennies until they've screamed. The real solution is increasing our revenues, and in making sure every dollar is spent as wisely as it can be.

I promised to talk more about tuition, and this is the time. Iowa provides us $4,013 for each of our students. Next year, we expect that 28 of "our" kids will choose to attend school in a neighboring district. That will cost us $112,364; we also pay $124,533 for 12 special education students receiving services outside our district. However, we more than make that money back with the $322,500 we take in from other districts. Still, if we were to convince half "our" students to stay in Mid-Prairie rather than open enroll out, or "borrow" another 14 kids from our neighbors, that would represent $56,000 a year in extra income, with next to no increase in our marginal costs of instruction.

While most educators are not trained to think like entrepreneurs, in an era when families have options, we have no choice but to put the best possible product on the market, and to let our "customers" know what we have to offer. Fifty-six thousand dollars buys lots of textbooks, and can also help us get our bank balance back where it needs to be in a hurry.

One final set of numbers from the income side of the balance sheet. Our proposed property tax levy for 2001 is $12.18 per thousand dollars assessed valuation. The equivalent levies were $12.28 in 2000, $12.92 in 1999, and $13.08 in 1998. Clearly, given that we've started rebuilding our Unspent Balance while tax rates have declined, we've taken the message of budgetary discipline to heart. It's hard to tell that to our current crop of students, though, when they're studying with outdated textbooks, taught by underpaid staff, and sitting in undermaintained buildings. The unavoidable reality is that if we must achieve an acceptable budgetary position through fiscal discipline alone, today's students won't be around to benefit when our district begins to reap the rewards.

None of us on the school board makes a nickel for our efforts. Our only compensation comes from trying to build better students and, by extension, a better future for us all. If you can help us in this endeavor, now is the time to share your observations and ideas. I've been told not to expect a crowd, but this is one budget issue for which I'd welcome a surprise.

FISCAL FITNESS

New Year's Day is when many of us resolve to get serious about physical fitness. We know that by eating right and exercising more, we'll look better, feel better and have a better chance of weathering any illnesses. Mid-Prairie has a similar goal—but instead of trying to cut pounds, we're trying to add heft to our bottom line.

Over the past half decade, we've seen our "Undesignated Unspent Balance" decline precipitously—from $523,528 in 1993 to $178,005 in 1998. Last year, due to the hard work and tough decisions of the previous board, we reversed that trend. By cutting spending and increasing fees, our balance jumped to $233,243. That's not where we want or need it to be, but for the first time in a half decade, the numbers are clearly heading in the right direction.

According to the Iowa Department of Education, a school district should have between 5 percent and 10 percent of its annual revenues socked away as its "Targeted Solvency Position." According to the state, "A school corporation with an Unreserved, Undesignated General Fund Balance equal to five to ten percent of actual revenues . . . is able to meet unforeseen financing requirements and presents a sound risk for the timely repayment of short-term debt obligations."

In our case, with $7,227,700 in annual receipts, a 5 percent ratio would mean having $361,385 in the bank with no strings attached, and a 10 percent ratio would mean $722,770. With our current balance, we're approximately $125,000 to $500,000 short of where we want to

be. To put it in more concrete terms, dividing our daily operating costs—
$39,745—into our total annual expenditures ($7,154,122 in 1998–1999),
we currently have 5.87 days' worth of spending in the bank.

While living the equivalent of paycheck-to-paycheck doesn't sound
wonderful, according to the state, we're at an "Acceptable Solvency Position"—a range that "should be considered adequate for short-term credit
purposes as long as other local economic trends, such as property tax col-
lections and enrollment, are sound. Continued close monitoring of the
school corporation budget to prevent operating shortfalls and the deterio-
ration of the financial position is necessary."

Continued close monitoring—and then some—is exactly what the
board has been doing. At our last meeting of 1999, we considered a proposal to restore funding for school field trips to its previous level. With
heavy hearts, we voted 5 to 2 to keep field trip funding for the entire
school district at $6,000—and not add the additional $6,000 that had been
proposed. While each of us recognizes the educational value of hands-on,
in-person learning, our existing field trip budget is only enough to send
each student to the equivalent of Iowa City twice each year for half-day
trips. It's not much, but for now, it's all the board thought we could afford.

Like a New Year's diet, sticking to a budget takes discipline, and we'd
be fooling ourselves if we didn't expect a fair amount of discomfort along
the way. As one of our three board goals this year, we formally resolved to
not spend money beyond that which we had budgeted, unless we identified
other funds to make up the difference. Because we could not identify
$6,000 of other spending that seemed less worthy, the field trips—and the
students who would have enjoyed and benefited from them—lost out.

When can we stop making these sacrifices? I know the board intends to
reverse the five-year decline in our bank account we experienced between
1993 and 1998, and suspect most of its members are committed to achieving at least a 5 percent—and preferably a 10 percent—cushion. With a
struggling farm economy and enrollments that declined in two-thirds of
Iowa districts this year, we simply need more than our current week's
worth of spending in the bank.

In the short-term, that means holding the line on spending, and in the
medium to long term, it probably means not implementing educational
priorities such as all-day everyday kindergarten. Equally unfortunately,
with a huge proportion of our budget linked to salaries, it also means

being less competitive than we would like in attracting the best and brightest new educators to the Mid-Prairie schools, and being less able to retain our most effective current employees.

Anyone who's gone on a diet knows there are two sides to the weight-loss equation—eat less and exercise more. Right now, all of us—members of the board, and particularly our students and staff—have personally experienced the hunger pangs resulting from our decreased consumption. My personal hope for the new year is that by demonstrating our ability to weather this discomfort, the community will choose to recognize our collective discipline, and will help us achieve our 5 percent to 10 percent cushion more rapidly through an increase in revenues.

There's no question we'll achieve "fiscal fitness" some day. What I worry about is how many field trips will never be taken, how many students will miss out on the lifelong benefits that a full-time kindergarten might bring, and how many educational initiatives will be squelched as we wait for that day to arrive.

FOOD FOR THOUGHT

A quarter century ago, Milton Friedman coined what might be the most famous expression in economics: "There's no such thing as a free lunch." The metaphor helped explain how economics works—we must make choices in life, and nothing comes without a cost.

As we sit here in August, just days before the new school year begins, that reality is becoming starkly clear in terms of a slightly different brand of economics: home economics.

If you've been reading the local papers, you're aware the wages Mid-Prairie is offering to kitchen employees—$6.74 for some positions to start—are apparently not sufficient to attract enough new workers to replace those who are leaving. If things don't change quickly, we literally may not have enough people to put lunch on our tables.

While he's famous for his "free lunch" line, Friedman won the 1976 Nobel Prize in Economics for his work explaining free markets. A 1932 college graduate, Friedman started his career during the Depression, and he spent most of the next half century working in times when most folks were happy to have jobs at all.

Needless to say, in the Year 2000 the free market tables have turned, as our school district is learning the hard way. With help wanted signs in every window, the modern choice isn't between a modest salary as a cook's helper or unemployment. The choice is between accepting an offer from us or from someone else—and we're in trouble if the grass is greener on the other prairie.

Other incentives—such as health benefits, a stress-free commute and the chance to work with nice people—can make a difference. Still, when it comes to recruiting new workers, the bottom line is usually the bottom line, and when it comes to hiring cooking staff, our bottom line is being spanked.

What do the current difficulties mean to our school district? To be honest, we're not sure. From a regulatory perspective, we are probably obligated to offer a school lunch program, and from a moral position, I think we have no other option.

Several times this year, we hear that for many of our students, the hot lunch they eat at school is their only well-balanced meal of the day. Our ability to provide free or reduced-price lunches—with the help of other government programs—enables those kids to forget their growling stomachs a few hours, and focus their attention on growing smarter.

Frankly, I'd rather see us spend our limited dollars on education than edibles, but as Friedman suggested, we live in an economy governed by market realities, not by magic wands. If we cannot attract enough people at lower wages, we may need to raise our pay to what economists call the "equilibrium point," the level at which supply meets demand.

To find the money to raise salaries, we may need to increase lunch prices, but simple math suggests that the money otherwise spent on two $9 pizzas could cover a ten cent price increase (from $1.50) for an entire year for a child with perfect attendance. We may also find that by limiting our range of lunch choices, we can increase staff efficiency, reducing our need for new workers. Still, I suspect we may have to bump up salaries a bit (or a few bits) to attract and retain good employees.

It's clear we cannot afford to keep on our present course. Last year, our recently departed middle school principal pulled several shifts on the lunch line when there was no one else to do the job. She's to be commended for pitching in, but we would be foolish if we didn't recognize that as a principal, she was awfully expensive help. To the extent her labors took her away from what we hired her to do, our savings represented a "false economy" in the truest sense of the term.

Milton Friedman has spent his life (88 years so far, and counting) sharing his passion for what many refer to as the "Dismal Science." But the lessons economics has to teach—that markets matter, a lot, and that there really is no such thing as a free lunch—are ones we can never afford to forget.

People who have the skills required to safely, efficiently and "tastefully" feed more than a thousand children each school day should be respected and, in a free market, fairly rewarded.

If we don't learn that lesson quickly, it will be our children who pay the price.

SPACE AGE MILEAGE, IRON AGE TRANSPORTATION

Thirty-six trips across the United States. Four treks around the world. An expedition that could take you halfway to the moon. No matter how you visualize it, with an average of 108,000 miles on the odometer, most Mid-Prairie school buses have a lot of miles under their belts, not to mention their shocks, bearings and bushings.

Mid-Prairie has 18 buses in its fleet, 12 in active service. Our average bus is 8 years old. The oldest joined our fleet about the same time as our seniors joined our world, back in 1983. Our spare buses, pressed into service when our regulars need maintenance, have contributed an average of 165,874 miles in service to our students.

While education is about teaching and learning, neither happens unless students get to school. In our district, that means a minimum of three years on the bus. If a kid lives in Kalona, he might stroll to school as a third-grader, but by the time he reaches high school, he won't be walking to Wellman. Likewise, a Wellman child might hike to class in her third or twelfth grades, but as a middle-school student, she'll be boarding the bus to Kalona.

Universal bus service has a huge impact on our budget. This year, our district has allocated $329,199 for transportation, or about $293 per student. Amazingly, that's less than the state average of $311, but enough to give our urban neighbors a decided advantage when it comes to balancing the budgetary demands of school buses and science books. Those numbers are also big enough that they may not mean much to the average reader. The average driver, though, knows what it means to see a car get older.

For example, each weekday I head down Highway 1 to Iowa City. While the 50 daily miles I drive seem like a lot, it's a third less than the 77 miles the average Mid-Prairie bus adds to its odometer. While I sometimes hardly even slow down on my way to work, Mid-Prairie buses make 25 to 30 stops each morning, and another 25 or 30 each afternoon. With the exception of my driveway, I don't see any gravel on my trip, while Mid-Prairie's buses drive half their miles on the rough stuff. Last but not least, I drive to work alone every day. I certainly don't carry 50 or more kids with an absolutely normal tendency to bounce up and down, slide side to side, and generally not behave like the passengers you might find in the business section of a 747.

I'm not as into cars as most guys, but after 60,000 highway miles, even I notice my Neon doesn't shine as brightly as when it came off the lot in 1996. I can only imagine what the toll might be if my car were twice as old with twice as many miles earned under much more challenging conditions, but the absolute reality is that's the kind of vehicle that we send our kids to school in every day.

Given the age of our transportation fleet, the school district is trying to keep up, but the miles—930 each day—add up more quickly than our dollars do. While we'd like to buy two buses each year, this year we've only been able to afford one—at $56,286 per copy. Consequently, our fleet's average age and mileage continue to increase, and the amount we can salvage from our old buses, in terms of both parts and potential sales, continues to decline.

While student transportation is required by state law, Iowa doesn't provide specialized funds to help us buy buses. We have to come up with the money, either as part of our regular budget, or from our Physical Plant and Equipment Levy funds.

Our current PPEL funding was authorized nearly a decade ago, and must be approved again by voters by next March to continue. If the PPEL fails, there's no denying our buses will grow less reliable. While regular maintenance can help forestall the inevitable, we can't ignore the fact that older buses will inevitably start to stall.

If we're lucky, stricken buses will never get out of the barn. If we're not, each unfortunate episode will mean a couple dozen kids stranded on a lonely gravel road inside a broken-down bus, and if it's in the morning, perhaps another couple dozen waiting along the route in the cold and dark. The alternative is shifting funds to buses from our instructional budget—that is, from books, teachers and field trips. At some point, of course, that becomes our only option.

By the way, our sturdiest steed, a 1987 model with a Ford Engine and a Bluebird body, had 250,707 miles on its odometer as of January 9. A quarter-million miles is nearly enough to take you to the moon, around the world AND across the United States.

And, as part of our active fleet, that bus probably carried 40 or 50 kids to school this morning.

THE BRAND NAME IN AMERICAN EDUCATION

Every year, Iowa's governor and key legislators address the Legislative Conference of the Iowa Association of School Boards. Most years, I suspect the assembled politicians attempt to outdo their peers in pledging their abiding allegiance to education. This year, though, I heard Governor Vilsack say he might deliver one-fourth of what he promised last year, and his Republican counterparts suggest we shouldn't count on that.

From this indistinguishable dialogue of doom, one phrase stuck with me. A Des Moines–area senator conceded Iowa's budget situation is awful, but contended we should pride ourselves that "Iowa is the brand name in American education."

She explained Iowa is the standard by which other state educational systems are judged. Our reputation, she said, was captured in the slogan: *Iowa—the SMART state for business.*

I may not be the sharpest pencil in Iowa's pocket, but I think the reason her statement stuck with me is that I haven't figured out her point. Was it that we shouldn't worry because our sparkling reputation will sustain us? Or was it that we must dig deep to protect Iowa's premier brand name from potentially irreparable damage?

Given that she wasn't pulling out her checkbook, I'm guessing her message was that we should ride on our reputation—and financial fumes—until we're more flush, and hope we don't run out of gas along the way.

Unfortunately for Iowa, sterling reputations can tarnish fast. In the business world, almost every week brings news of the downfall of another American icon. Among the recent casualties is Kmart, which has declared Chapter 11. According to the smart-money guys on Wall Street, the company couldn't find a profitable niche (read reputation) between low-priced Wal-Mart and cheap-and-chic Target.

Similarly, if you've ever wanted a Lincoln Continental, buy it now. Because of Ford's misbegotten corporate makeover, its former marquee model is biting the dust. (If you've ever ached for an Escort, don't dawdle either. That brand is also a goner.)

Of course, the biggest brand debacle belongs to Enron. Its business model depended upon trust; when that went away, its black ink bled red. Arthur Andersen, its Big Five accounting firm, is boiling in the same pot of hot water. The day this was written a web headline blared, *Delta may oust Andersen as auditor: Airline searching for replacement in wake of Enron fiasco.*

According to MSNBC, FedEx is also "assessing its relationship with Andersen, which goes back at least 20 years (and) BB&T, the nation's 16th-largest banking company, said Andersen's business with the company is up for review after a 36-year relationship." University of Chicago accounting expert Ray Ball added, "It's a brave CEO who's willing to get on board with Andersen at the moment. . . . It would be very difficult to get that through the board and stockholders because of the reputation effect."

One reason I write this column is to create a positive and persistent mental association (read reputation) with the Mid-Prairie school district. Just as we've learned Apple wants us to *Think Different,* IBM wants us to embrace *e-business* and a guy in an elf suit wants us to tell our kids, *Dude, you're getting a Dell!* I want us to think "Mid-Prairie" when we think about the state's best school district—and I want Americans to think the same thing about Iowa education.

Reputation, though, isn't enough. Think of the brands that used to be household names in your house. A&P. Montgomery Ward. FW Woolworth. If the "five-and-dimes" can fade away, it's time to seriously consider the risk of Iowa's schools getting nickel-and-dimed not to death, but to mediocrity, in our admittedly grim economic environment.

How do we protect our good name? Sure, we can talk ourselves up, but reputation ultimately rests on reality—and the truth is that we must invest dollars (and sweat equity) in our schools today if we want Iowa education to survive as the gold standard a generation from now.

One short year ago, Enron was the seventh largest corporation in America, worth tens of billions of dollars. We're fooling ourselves, but few others, if we think we can ride solely on our reputation for long.

HATFIELDS, MCCOYS AND HAWKEYES

A century ago, the Hatfields and McCoys waged a feud that still lives in the American imagination. Despite their storied history, the clans recently put aside their differences, and two years ago celebrated their first combined family reunion, at which the most pitched battles took place on a softball field.

Although we're far from the foggy mountains of Appalachia, Iowans are no strangers to long-term hostilities. For better or worse, our differences still help define who we are.

If you want evidence for that assertion, ask an Iowan if they support Iowa or Iowa State. In some parts, just asking could earn you a bloody nose.

Unfortunately, the animosity not only runs across higher learning, but up and down our educational infrastructure. When Iowa's "Regent Institutions" had their budgets slashed in the last legislative session, were we—as elementary or secondary school leaders—picking up cudgels to fight on behalf of our fellow educators, for our recent graduates now in college, or for the young men and women who will soon be our teachers and taxpayers?

Not that I noticed.

Similarly, when we went to Des Moines seeking budgetary benevolence, did the university presidents stand at our sides and tell legislators that their schools depend upon our success in producing students worthy of college admission?

If they did, it again escaped my attention.

Finally, when the Department of Human Services asked for permission to stop tracking truants for one year, did we—as local educators—lobby on DHS's behalf since their fight against truancy was really our fight to keep kids in schools?

I know I didn't, and if anyone else did, I missed that too.

Earlier this year, I had the opportunity to speak with the leaders of a state educational group. Given our symbiotic interests, I asked, "Have we considered more cooperative lobbying with Iowa's universities or community colleges?" To be honest, I don't remember their exact answer, but I do recall them looking at me as if I had three heads.

That's too bad, because if we were to tell legislators a well-documented story describing how we work together to advance learning in Iowa, my guess is they'd listen. Even if they didn't, simply by talking to each other we might learn something, which has its own rewards.

For evidence of that assertion, you don't have to look farther than Des Moines—an admittedly hard thing for us downstate denizens to swallow.

This summer, Iowa and Iowa State, along with the University of Northern Iowa, Drake University, Grand View College, Simpson College and Des Moines Area Community College will break ground on a $6 million *Gateway Center*. The 40,000 square-foot, four-story building will not only be home to programs from Iowa's "Seven Sisters" of higher education, but to training programs from leading local businesses. Even better, rather than wasting money on redundant resources, it will use computers at a nearby library instead of insisting upon its own infrastructure.

With that much talent aligned to deliver outstanding educational programs, the "Higher Education Collaborative" can hardly help but be successful.

One last feud story. As an Iowa City kid, the only time I thought about Cedar Rapids was when the aroma from its cereal mills wafted in our direction.

This month, leaders from Cedar Rapids, Iowa City and eight other governments signed a joint proclamation in which they agreed to cooperatively market Iowa's *Technology Corridor*.

According to Charlie Funk of the Iowa City Area Development Group, as quoted in the *Cedar Rapids* (or is it *Iowa City*?) *Gazette*: "The bottom line is we're all working together. That doesn't necessarily mean that we will stop competing for businesses. We will be aboveboard in our dealings with each other. We will work for the good of the region as a whole."

As the Hatfields and McCoys learned, it's more fun throwing softballs to each other than brickbats at each other. Up and down the line, Iowa's schools were bloodied in this year's budget battles. It might be a good learning experience to see how we'd fare if we were all playing for the same team.

A PIOUS AND EXEMPLARY COMMUNITY

'Tis the season for New Year's resolutions. In accordance with custom, many of us will begin 2002 resolved that this will be the year we finally transform our bodies from ground round to buff beef.

Unfortunately, there's also an unforgiving gauge of our success in doing so. Although crude devices, we buy "scales" knowing their sole purpose is to display numbers that, over time, tell us whether we're heading in the right direction.

The numbers don't lie, but should we find ourselves heading the wrong way, we'll convince ourselves we're "big-boned," or so fit our massive muscles go unappreciated by simple measures such as "pounds." We'll substitute height-and-weight charts with Body Mass Indexes, hoping higher math delivers better news. If it doesn't, we may buy calipers to measure our folds of (ahem) skin, or even weigh ourselves underwater to better "get the skinny" on our excess insulation.

Even if bad news consistently floats to the top, we'll try to stay the course in our food and fitness regimes because, in our heart-of-hearts, we know it's good for us. Only the strongest-willed among us, though, will keep stepping on scales, because the unblinking mechanical monsters have a regrettable tendency to tell us what we don't want to hear.

In education, the obvious corollary to "pounds" is performance on standardized tests, including all the resentments. Confirmation comes from the biggest applause line at this fall's Iowa Association of School Boards conference, when a speaker proclaimed: "You don't fatten a hog by weighing it more often."

True, but if you're purchasing a pig, you want to know how much ham to expect for your hard-earned dollars. For better or worse, as we move into the new year, the United States will be paying far more attention to our educational scales than ever before.

In one of its last acts of 2001, the U.S. Senate overwhelmingly approved the Elementary and Secondary Education Act. In the words of one legislator, ESEA made comrades of congressmen who "spent their careers throwing rocks at each other." Sen. Edward Kennedy, nobody's conservative, called ESEA "a blueprint for progress in all of the nation's schools."

The $26.5 billion act requires annual reading and math tests for all 3rd through 8th graders, with the results broken down by the race, gender and economic background of the students. Poorly performing schools must devote federal dollars to tutoring struggling students, or even send their kids to other, "better" public schools. President Bush claims ESEA will create "real accountability, unprecedented flexibility for states and school districts, greater local control, more options for parents and more funding for what works."

This is only an educated guess, but I suspect ESEA, also known as the *No Child Left Behind Act*, will have little short-term impact on Mid-Prairie.

We already test our kids every year, and it's unlikely we'll land on a hit list of underperforming schools. As journalist Philip Terzian writes, "(Bush's) education package tends to concentrate on those who need it: Failing students and systems with large numbers of poor children. . . . (Missing) are students who are doing relatively well in school, and those districts that have sufficient resources to support them. The federal government doesn't have much to offer here."

Still, the act will undeniably usher in a new era in Iowa education. Before ESEA, Iowa alone did not impose state standards on its schools, believing those were best left to local boards. Post-ESEA, Mid-Prairie may not have state mandates, but we will have federal ones.

Iowa's previous policy does afford us one unique advantage. Alone among the 50 states, we'll start with a clean slate, which is also the foremost benefit to a New Year's resolution, as Mark Twain noted in 1863: "Yesterday, everybody smoked his last cigar, took his last drink, and swore his last oath. Today, we are a pious and exemplary community."

Truth is, educators are an exemplary community. As with any human institution, we are not perfect, but most of the time we're heading in the right direction. That should make it easier, at least a little bit, when it comes time to step up on the scale.

COUNT NOSES—DON'T PICK THEM

If you're like most folks, you occasionally look around and wonder how the local landscape appeared one hundred years ago, before so many people lived here.

I enjoyed such daydreams until I discovered Washington County, home to most of the Mid-Prairie district, actually had slightly MORE people a century ago than it did in the most recent census—20,712 in 1900 compared with 20,670 in 2000.

Iowa's total population increased over the same span, from 2.2 million to 2.9 million, but a select few urban centers carried the demographic ball, with just six counties covering the entire net gain. According to Iowa State University Census Services, 24 other counties also picked up a few folks, but 69 counties had fewer inhabitants at the end of century than they did at its beginning.

Interest in Iowa's demographic destiny spiked recently, when it was reported that after a decade with solid 5.4 percent growth, Iowa's population slipped during the 15 months following the April 2000 enumeration. The state is contesting the count, but no matter how you slice it, it's undeniable Iowa's population is stagnant at best, shrinking at worst, and that there are pockets — large, nearby pockets — whose populations are plummeting.

For example, Keokuk County, our neighbor to the west, found little to cheer about as it lost residents for ten straight decades. In absolute numbers, it came in dead last among Iowa's 99 counties, with its robust 1900 headcount of 24,979 dwindling to 11,624 souls as we turned the corner into the new millennium.

Seven counties fared even worse in relative terms. Southwest Iowa's Adams County "led" that pitiable pack by losing more than 67 percent of its population. In other words, if you were in a group photo with three people in 1900, you'd literally be "the only one left in the picture" by 2000.

What that means for school districts is obvious. With about $4,500 in state funds riding on each enrollment, it's tempting to imagine little dollar signs running around playgrounds instead of little kids. Fortunately, Mid-Prairie's census has been stable, hovering around 1,250 in recent years. How do we ensure our population, in and out of its schools, stays at least the same?

In an editorial titled "Let Population Loss be Catalyst for Action," the *Iowa City Gazette* recommends plugging the "brain drain" that results in Iowa's college graduates leaving the state for "greener" climes. It specifically mentioned graduating education students (i.e., new teachers), whom we seem to grow — and export — almost as successfully as we do corn.

The paper also recommends welcoming legal immigrants. It observes that a century ago, Iowa "was teeming with immigrants and ready to thrive. Once safely in, though, newcomers typically want to seal off the borders." As noted, in 69 counties the natives have "succeeded" all too well. Governor Vilsack wants to add 310,000 Iowans by 2010, but amazingly, his foes see Vilsack's red carpet as a red flag that will help unseat him in this fall's election.

What should truly scare the "loser" counties is another idea that's picking up steam, namely, saving "costs by consolidating small counties and school districts." For marginal local entities, this is where the rubber hits the road. When a "winner" such as Johnson County (up 347 percent for the century) can have courthouse jobs threatened by a state seeking to stream-line government, no agency dependent upon state funds can rest easy.

One of my favorite bumper stickers reads, *There are three kinds of people in this world: Those who can count, and those who can't.* Rest assured, the public servants who create budgets can count—people, votes, students and dollars.

If we hope to survive, and thrive, through the end of this century, we must make our rural areas as vibrant and inviting as our urban sectors, and there's no better way to do that than through our schools.

If we fail to meet that challenge, no one should be surprised when (not if) we have far fewer people populating the local landscape in 2100 than we did way back in 2002.

Chapter Eight

Politics

BELIEVE IN FAMILY VALUES? PROVE IT

If you want your children to be enthusiastic readers and writers throughout their lives, you don't start them reading and writing at age 18.

If you want your children to be world-class athletes or musicians, you don't wait until they graduate from high school to hand them their first basketball or violin.

If you want your children to practice religion as adults, you don't leave them at home on Sunday while you pray at your church alone.

Yet, while most of us want our kids to become upstanding citizens, we disenfranchise them from the most fundamental aspect of civic participation—voting. Perhaps as a result, it takes years for most young adults to find their ways to the polls.

How do you fix that? Simple. You let kids vote. Sound outrageous? Before dismissing the idea, look at how the lack of universal suffrage distorts our politics.

Before this week's election, both Al Gore and George W. Bush pledged to help senior citizens pay for prescription drugs and to safeguard Social Security. While they had different solutions, neither was reluctant to spend tax dollars make their ideas real.

Much further down the radar screen were federal support for schools and health care for children. While both candidates discussed these issues, you didn't see either stand at a schoolhouse door proclaiming, "I don't care what it costs. Education now! Health care forever!"

If America's 60 million minor children had the right to vote, or if their parents had their proxies, would the political calculus change? In a heartbeat.

Not only would speeches be made, but funding would be found—and in the process, children might discover the power politics has to improve people's lives, particularly their own.

How might children's suffrage work? Obviously, infants can't vote by themselves, and even adolescents might need assistance. However, newborns could receive both birth and voting certificates at the hospital, and older children voter registration forms at school. The trick is not making children eligible, but making sure their votes count.

That's where education kicks in. Today, it's not uncommon for students to participate in mock elections at school—but after the votes come in, we pat our kids on the head and tell them (whether or not we say it out loud), "That's nice, but what you think doesn't really count."

Kids may be young, but they aren't stupid. After a few years, they learn it's best not to care too much about electoral outcomes, because they don't matter anyway. As any coach could tell you, if you practice something often enough, behaviors become internalized to the point you don't even have to think about them any more—and judging by our abysmal voter participation rate, we've been wildly successful in that regard.

How about injecting real family values into politics, as defined by family voting? For children to exercise their franchise, a parent would have to join them in the polling booth, where together they would cast votes that really count.

Like weekly church attendance, regular voting would get our kids into the habit of civic participation, even if they don't understand everything that's going on. Even if parents are the ones pulling the levers, casting ballots on their children's behalf and in their presence might force them to think of the long-term good of our larger society, another laudable outcome.

However, children won't stay silent long. By kindergarten, they'll want to know what they're doing, and parents can deliver their first lecture on civic responsibility. By 3rd grade, discussions can be held about the merits of various candidates, and through the prodding of their schools, the children might play an important role in dragging their parents to the polls.

By the time they hit high school, discussions might evolve into debates. For kids' votes to count, parent and child must resolve any differences to the extent both agree to show up to vote—which would again pay dividends beyond the immediate ballot.

Within my grandparents' lifetimes, women's suffrage became a reality, and within my lifetime, black people earned voting rights. Although men and white folks lost power as a result, "giving" these two groups the vote was clearly the right thing to do.

Today, the only group disenfranchised at birth are children. That affects not only today's governmental priorities, but undermines the future vitality of our democracy.

I'm not crazy enough to think my children will vote as children, but my grandchildren might. It will erode my vote and yours, but it's the right thing to do.

REALLY NOTHING OUTRAGEOUS

While state funding is clearly Iowa's K–12 education story of 2002, it might not be the one we talk about in 2012. Budgets go up and down, but I've never seen a proposal attempting to slay as many sacred cows as the *Education Accountability Act of 2002*.

Rep. Jack Hatch, a Des Moines Democrat, introduced the bill. Acknowledging it would go nowhere this year, Hatch nonetheless told the media, "We have to go forward. This is a massive project, and we have got to get some discussion about this."

"The education establishment will not be pleased with the recommendations or the statistics," concurred Rep. Chuck Larson, chair of the Iowa GOP. "But reform is needed. Iowa parents will be very, very pleased."

The source of this curious consensus was a devastating report by the State of Black Iowa Initiative. The underlying study surveyed every Iowa school district and the top 20 employers in each county. It found, for example, that 78 percent of black 8th graders in Davenport did not read at proficient levels, 60 percent of Iowa's black children under 5 lived in poverty, and 17 percent of jailed juveniles are black—five times their proportion of the population.

"This is not a pleasant document," said Jonathan Narcisse, president of the Initiative and publisher of the *Iowa Bystander,* the oldest African American newspaper west of the Mississippi. "It represents a tragic truth we have been loath to accept."

What makes the report so interesting is that Narcisse doesn't want Iowa to feel sorry for its minority citizens—or to single out black kids for more attention. Instead, he wants us to strengthen our standards for all our students, knowing that long-term opportunity lies in academic accomplishment.

"If you read the legislation, you know it isn't race-specific," said Narcisse. "This focuses on accountability and responsibility. There is really nothing outrageous that we've proposed."

Outrage, though, might lie in eye of the beholder. Among other things, the bill targets truancy. After a semester's second unexcused absence, "a warning will be issued by the county prosecutor's office, and, if appropriate, DHS." Perhaps even more draconian, dropouts could lose driving privileges until their class graduates.

The bill's just as tough on schools, shifting funding from an enrollment- to an attendance-based formula. "Schools will maintain attendance records by day and by class/period. . . . Up to five excused absences per semester will be allowed prior to adjusting student compensation. No unexcused absences will be compensated."

To ensure data aren't manipulated, the bill calls for uniform definitions. Narcisse notes the official Iowa dropout rate is 1.74 percent, and about twice that for African Americans—but also that some reports suggest nearly half Iowa's black kids don't finish high school. What gives?

Using the state's own data (*Annual Condition of Education, 2000*), I crunched some numbers. Tracking the same groups of kids from 1998–1999 to 1999–2000, enrollments for the grades 9 to 10, 10 to 11 and 11 to 12 cohorts fell 3.84 percent, 4.60 percent, and 3.01 percent, respectively.

For grades 1–8, on the other hand, the worst performance is a 0.09 percent decrease from grades 1 to 2, and the best is a 2.48 percent increase from grades 6 to 7. Clearly, family emigration from Iowa isn't the problem—but it still appears kids are leaving high school at twice the official dropout rate. I guess those are the ones "falling through the cracks."

Finally, if Narcisse's numbers don't scare you, try this on for size. "(The initiative) also plans to . . . look at the feasibility of changing the state's public education system to serving children ages 3 to 16 rather than ages 5 to 18, with juniors and seniors being served by community colleges." That should get your attention.

"This report is an extraordinarily good piece of work," said Hatch. "It raises significant policy issues that cannot be ignored."

So far, though, the Legislature has done just that. The Act died this year during the funnel process, and the Iowa Association of School Boards' website doesn't even mention it as worth tracking.

Still, in Davenport (home of the 22 percent reading rate), Superintendent Jim Blanche told Narcisse he was "interested in working with him. Anything that can improve the education of our students would be wonderful."

Very, very pleased. Nothing really outrageous. Extraordinarily good work. Wonderful.

Remember, when 2012 rolls around, you read it here first.

PPEL FORUM DRAWS NEAR

Earlier this year, the Mid-Prairie School Board decided to back off from an early vote on the Physical Plant and Equipment Levy (PPEL). Our decision to delay the referendum wasn't made because the PPEL, which runs out in 2001, isn't needed. The reason we chose to wait is so we could take the time to clearly communicate our schools' needs to the people who will determine the outcome of the vote. In other words, you.

The first major step in the outreach effort will occur Wednesday at the Middle School. The Mid-Prairie Foundation has sent letters to local leaders encouraging them to attend the meeting—along with any members, neighbors or friends they know who are willing to invest 90 minutes in discussing the future of our schools.

As board members, we're following up on those letters with phone calls this week, again asking for participation. We want to do what we can to get out the word that everyone—whether or not they ultimately expect to cast their votes for the PPEL—is strongly encouraged to attend.

At the meeting, we will present a 25- to 30-minute overview of the PPEL. The presentation will explain what needs the levy would address—including transportation, energy efficiency, building security, health and safety, building repair, and equipment replacement. It will explain how much the items in each of those categories are expected to cost over the next decade, and from what sources the revenues can be raised to address these concerns.

The presentation will describe the PPEL in the context of a rural school district with five instructional buildings, each of which is well into its "middle-aged" years. It will explain how we currently replace our school buses once every 240,000 miles, and how, even with the PPEL, we have earmarked only $20,000 per year for instructional technology—or less than $20 per student per year despite the fact we are just now entering the first of what are sure to be many "dot.com" decades to come.

From there, we'll explain how the PPEL works—how much funding we're talking about, how the level of the levy gets set, and where the revenue can come from. The reason I wrote "how the level of the levy gets set" is that as a board member, I can honestly report we have not set that level yet. We want to get your comments first so that we can send to the voters a PPEL you believe is consistent with our district's needs and resources.

At that point, we want to quit talking and start listening. We want to know whether you think our list is complete, whether you think we've put too much on it, or even whether you think we ought to pay for our schools' tuckpointing out of the textbook budget.

We're also looking for policy direction. In the past, the board has authorized a matching funding program. With matching funds, an organization can raise money for a permanent project to benefit the schools with an expectation of help from the board. We want to know whether you think that program ought to be re-established—or whether you think it's more important to work through our list first.

From my perspective, it's not an easy call, because I know how serious many of our physical plant and equipment needs are. But before I cast any votes on the issue, I want to hear from people who have ideas that could move our schools to the next level of excellence. That's why we all ran for the board, and what everyone wants for our schools.

Finally, after listening carefully to the comments, questions and ideas, and providing answers where we can, we'll work with you to determine what must occur over the next few months to turn the community's wishes into reality. Among the items we expect to see on our "To-Do List" are setting a date for the potential referendum, determining a proposed levy, and creating committees to help tell people what the PPEL means to our schools and our community at large.

While we always welcome your input, if people don't voice their opinions at school board meetings, we can always do what you elected us to do—use our collective judgment to make the best use of the resources we have available for our schools. At the forum, though, we can't succeed unless cross-sections of the several communities that constitute our school district contribute to the discussion.

Your participation in the PPEL forum can help ensure that happens. We want to do right by you, our schools and our students. We welcome your participation in the process.

YOUR WALLET—AND YOUR WISDOM

This Wednesday we're asking you to make a special one-hour visit to the Mid-Prairie Middle School in Kalona to attend a public forum on our district's physical plant and equipment needs.

This meeting is your chance to hear from representatives of our school system about what we're doing to ensure our facilities and equipment are ready for a new century of learning. More important, it's our chance to hear from you about your priorities for our buildings, grounds and equipment, and about how much you think we—as a community—ought to pay for them.

Keeping our infrastructure in shape for the 1,250 students and 180 adults who use our facilities 180 days each year is a daunting task. While you can imagine what it would be like to have hundreds of kids tromp through your house each day for 30 or 40 years, a quick statistical tour of our school district also helps to describe the challenges we face.

The Senior High School in Wellman, originally constructed in 1962, now contains 49 rooms spread out over 89,130 square feet. The Middle School in Kalona, built in 1969, has 47 rooms and 43,427 square feet.

Our three elementary schools date from the 1950s, 1960s and 1970s. Kalona Elementary, with 44 rooms and 30,238 square feet, started out slightly more than a third of its present size in 1955. Washington Township, constructed in 1964, has 17,856 square feet spread out among 25 rooms. Wellman Elementary opened for business in 1978, and has 38 rooms and 17,856 square feet of space.

The grand total of rooms is 203, and the total square footage is 212,255. Those are a lot of rooms and square feet to keep heated, ventilated and protected from the elements, but it's a cost we simply cannot wish away.

The replacement value of our buildings is $14,708,206, if they're empty. Add the costs of carpets and floor tiles for our students to walk on (most are more than 25 years old), furniture for them to sit on (more than a $2 million investment), equipment for them to learn with (both chalkboards and computers), and buses to get them back and forth from home, and the size of our existing investment becomes increasingly difficult to ignore. To steal from former Senator Everett Dirksen, "A million dollars here and a million dollars there, and pretty soon you're talking about real money."

Now, add in our immediate maintenance needs (cracking asphalt, leaking roofs, tuckpointing, painting, sewer line repairs and inadequate handicapped access), and a sampling of the short- to medium-term items (an aging transportation fleet, heating and cooling upgrades, unlockable lockers, and what should be a replacement schedule for desks, chairs, other furniture and instructional equipment), and it's easy to see why we believe this is an issue that deserves our community's focused attention.

That's where you come in. In life, we all must make choices, and our schools are no different. We wish we had an unlimited bank account to address all our needs, both present and future, but we don't and never will. Given that reality, we need to know your opinions regarding what our priorities should be, and how much we should be willing to invest to make them happen. With that information, together we can construct a plan for maintaining and improving our schools that will not only help our students learn in the short term, but reflect well on our communities for decades to come.

To be perfectly honest, our schools cannot make it without your support, but just as important as your wallet is your wisdom. We'll be directly soliciting community leaders as well as members of school groups to participate in this forum, but we want everyone with an interest in our schools and their funding to attend—and if you've read this far, that obviously includes you.

See you there.

WE THE PPEL

In just two months, the Physical Plant and Equipment Levy will go before Mid-Prairie voters. The PPEL (sounds like *pebble*) is money earmarked for the upkeep and updating of our educational infrastructure—the buildings, buses, desks and other durable goods we need to get our kids to school and keep them learning.

Although many of us are concentrating on baseball's pennant races this time of year, this is also the political season—and the September PPEL vote will arrive long before the World Series. As in baseball, the moves made now, during the dog days of summer, will determine whether we coast to the finish, or scrap for every vote come referendum day—and as any manager can tell you, any team that tries to coast is "toast."

A quick history of the PPEL. Ten years ago, Mid-Prairie voters approved the current PPEL—a levy that expires on June 30, 2001. This spring, after receiving public input at meetings in May and June, the school board set the proposed PPEL renewal at $1.20, with a no more than 6 percent surtax on state income taxes, and PPEL property tax of approximately 41 cents per thousand dollars assessed valuation.

While the new PPEL of $1.20, on paper, is larger than our current levy of 67 cents, the cost of our debt service is also going down. The net result for most taxpayers is that if the PPEL passes, the overall cost of supporting our schools will almost be a wash. PPEL revenues will rise slightly, other taxes will slightly decline, and the total outlay will stay about the same. It's also worth noting that no matter how you slice it, our overall school-based property taxes are still a relative bargain at $12.18—more than a dollar cheaper than our regional average, and a full five dollars less than some of our neighbors.

What will change is our ability to keep our schools safe and service-able. Our current PPEL raises $189,000 a year—not nearly enough to maintain our 90,000 square feet of building space, keep our buses on a reasonable replacement schedule (at current rates, we're trading them in at the 250,000 mile mark), or keep pace with the technologies our students must master if they expect to prosper in the century to come.

A few examples illustrate what we're up against. A year ago I had no idea what "tuckpointing" was. Now I know it means to restore defective mortar in brickwork—and that a six-year-old estimate for tuckpointing at the Middle School alone ran $50,000.

The cost of doing nothing is letting water wash into the building, having it freeze and thaw, and then letting even more water in the next year. At some point, tuckpointing takes precedence over textbooks and teachers—with the real cost being paid by our students in the short term, and our community in the long term.

Not only are some walls crumbling, so are some ceilings. At the Middle School and at Kalona Elementary, a quick glance overhead confirms the sorry condition of the ceiling tiles. Many have long ago fallen down—and those that remain may be even more problematic. In Kalona's 4th/5th-grade pod, molds are growing on the backsides of stained ceiling tiles, but it doesn't do much good to replace the tiles if the roof lets even more water seep in—yet another reason PPEL funds are needed.

The new PPEL will raise approximately $328,000 a year. We've identified about $3,140,000 in projected PPEL expenditures over the next decade without factoring in inflation or the repairs that we don't know about—or about $314,000 per year. In passing the $1.20 levy, the consensus of the board was that the $14,000 annual difference between the expected revenues and expenditures should be set aside to provide the infrastructure for all-day everyday kindergarten, a long-term goal this board is committed to achieving.

Early July is not only the time we settle in for baseball's All-Star game, it's also when we celebrate the wisdom of our founders. Their sacrifices gave us taxation WITH representation and, by extension, many of the liberties and privileges—including universal public education—we take for granted today.

Baseball is our national pastime, but education is our nation's future. Please make sure you're ready to step up to the plate and vote.

THE NUMBERCRUNCHERS

Norman and Penelope Numbercruncher live in the hypothetical hamlet of Math Fork, halfway between here and there.

"We got married on 9/25/64—the last square day of the 1960s," laughs Norm. "Three times three equals nine, five times five equals 25, and eight times eight equals 64. I've always had a head for figures, and being married on a square day to a woman with a figure like Penny's—well, it just added up."

Norm and Penny enjoy a good life in Math Fork. They raised four children, all of whom graduated from the local schools. While Norm's nuts for numbers, it's Penny who counts every dollar coming through their home. They've paid off the mortgage on what is now a $100,000 house, and live comfortably on their combined $34,000 income.

"I'm sorry to see my kids leave the nest," sighs Penny, "but they turned out OK, and I sure enjoy being a grandmother."

While Norm runs a looser financial ship ("There's only one Penny I like to pinch," he laughs), they both know a dollar is more easily spent than earned. That's why, when they came to last week's public forum on the Physical Plant and Equipment Levy, they went in with their minds open—but their eyes focused on the bottom line.

They listened as the district outlined $3,144,000 in projected physical plant and equipment spending over the years 2001 to 2011. That's the money required to update the bus fleet, repair aging buildings, replace deteriorating lockers and desks, increase energy efficiency, and provide a little extra— $200,000 over the decade—for equipment directly related to instruction.

"Three million dollars," whispered Penny. "That's a lot of money."

"Well," said Norm, tapping his pencil, "that's over 10 years, so it's $314,400 annually. The $200,000 for instructional equipment works out to $20,000 per year. Divide that by 1,250 students, and that's $16 per student per year. Even pinching pennies, you can't buy much of a computer with that."

"But who's going to come up with the $3 million?" Penny insisted. "You don't like taxes any more than I do."

Norm studied the district's spreadsheet, scribbled a few more figures, and started thinking aloud.

"Let's see. The existing PPEL raises $179,509 a year. We have a 4 percent income tax surtax that brings in $144,837, and we get the other $34,672 from property taxes. With the 54.85 percent property tax rollback on our $100,000 house, that means we pay less than $6.47 in PPEL property taxes and, with our income, about $33.50 a year in surtax. That puts us at about $40 a year right now.

"Now, if the PPEL levy were to increase to $1.20 from the current 67 cents, that would generate the $314,400 the district needs, but what would it do to our taxes? If the surtax went from 4 percent to 6 percent, that would mean a $16.75 increase in income taxes. That would leave another $13.25 to be made up by the property tax—about $30 in all, or less than a dime a day."

"Thirty dollars? That's about the cost of last night's pizza party," said Penny. "Still, I'm don't want to spend extra on anything if I don't have to."

"Penny, let's say that pizza is our income. The part that goes to the PPEL now is one-tenth of one percent of what we bring in. Divide a 14-inch pizza into 1,000 slices, and the PPEL slice is 1/25 of an inch wide. Even I wouldn't miss that from a 14-inch pizza."

Penny pondered her husband's calculations, and then whispered back.

"Norm, I think you got the right answer the wrong way."

Intrigued, Norm listened.

"Last fall, Norm Junior turned down a fancy job in a big city because he didn't want his kids to go to schools where the roofs leaked and the walls crumbled. If the schools start falling apart here, he might make a different decision next time.

"And if Junior leaves, not only do our grandkids live somewhere else, but the money Mid-Prairie gets from the state goes somewhere else. I'm not the mathematician here, but with the $4,500 the district gets for each student, it would take 150 of our $30 increases to make up the difference for each one of his kids. With three children, Normie's decision to stay is the same as having 450 families paying the extra PPEL levy.

"Plus, if Junior moves out and new families don't move in, the housing market gets soft, real estate valuations go down, and the tax rates for everything—public safety, sewers, parks, libraries and schools—need to make up the difference. We're talking about more than a sliver of pizza!"

Norman and Penelope returned to Math Fork, pleased to have worked through the figures for themselves. They resolved to get to the polls when the PPEL appeared on the ballot, and called Norm Junior and his family to come over for pizza the next evening.

The Numbercrunchers expected it would only be the first of many such parties over the years to come.

PRIMER ON PROPER GOVERNANCE

It's been said that since the U.S. Constitution was ratified two centuries ago, every other country in the world has been turned upside down, but one—ours—remains rightside up. The reason is not that we're smarter than everyone else. More likely, we simply have the good fortune to live a country where the system works.

Sure, there are some malcontents—me included—quick to point out our shortcomings. That said, the undeniable truth is that when a society allows individual energies and ideas to play themselves out in an environment characterized by both freedom and the rule of law, its people flourish.

As this article is being written, the school election is several days away. I don't know who will be joining the school board, and I don't know if the PPEL levy has passed or failed. What I do know is that since classes let out last spring, more than half the board has turned over and, by next summer, we'll have a wholly new superintendent.

The changes don't worry me, though, because like America, our district is governed by principles that speak more eloquently, and forcefully, than any of the people who happen to work on its behalf. Simply put, those governance principles are 1) the board makes policy, 2) the administration carries out policy, and 3) you provide the wisdom and energy that underlie everything we do. But for our system to work as it should, each of us must understand our roles within it.

Let's start with concerns about our schools. If you think a policy is not being followed, the first (and usually most effective) place to state your case is with the employee closest to the situation, usually a teacher, coach or other member of the front-line staff. If you are still not satisfied, go up the ladder to the principal, and if you're still not happy, the next stop is the superintendent's office.

While it may seem like passing the buck, it is generally best not to start with a board member, because while we're "in charge," we can't overrule staff decisions, and it would be terrible if we could.

Imagine a disgruntled parent going from board member to board member seeking "justice" for his child. Then suppose I intervened, righting the alleged wrong. A second board member sees things the opposite way, though, and "decrees" a different solution. There are still five members to go, but already, chaos reigns. Not good.

That said, if you don't like a bad policy, or think we're missing the boat on a great opportunity, you should contact a board member, or better yet, speak to all the board at one of our meetings. For example:

If you believe that all-day everyday kindergarten is an educational bonanza or an economic boondoggle, tell us. We're the ones who have to start it up or shoot it down.

If you believe one weekday evening and every Sunday should be reserved for family and church, and that school events should never be scheduled at those times, tell us. We're the ones who can set those times aside, or make them available.

If you think we place too much, or too little, emphasis on certain extracurricular or academic endeavors, tell us. We're the ones who decide who gets money and who goes without.

While sound in principle, a solid structure is not bulletproof. If I try to throw my weight around in the schools (and people are foolish enough to pay attention), or if the administration refuses to adhere to board policies, the system breaks down. Similarly, if the board and administration aren't working as a team, good governance grinds to a halt.

A system of checks and balances is not always efficient, in Washington, D.C., or in Wellman, Iowa. Still, over the course of history, this structure has served our country, and district, well, and I am confident it will do so in the future.

And, as always, if you have a better idea, tell us.

AN ACT OF POLITICAL HERESY

I'm about to commit a tiny act of political heresy, so brace yourself. Most times I come across a *Get Out the Vote* campaign, I secretly hope it fails.

It's not that I'm against broad-based participation in our democracy. On the contrary, I'm all for long lines at the voting booth. What troubles me is the potential dilution of my vote by yahoos whose impetus for political involvement may be a 15-second TV spot by Madonna, literally wrapped in the flag, threatening to "spank" anyone who doesn't get to the polls.

That's why you should make sure your vote counts next Tuesday. By reading this far into the column, you've demonstrated that before voting, you take the time to carefully consider the people and issues that will appear on the ballot—and that's exactly the kind of participation we need to make our democracy work.

Unlike the citizens-by-sound-bite who look to celebrities for civic inspiration (fortunately, I suspect there are few who actually make it to the voting booth), I trust that your judgment, combined with mine and that of all our fellow sober-minded citizens, will result in government leaders and policies that will serve us well.

In this election, we'll be choosing from among five write-in candidates (as this is being written) for three wide-open board positions, one listed candidate whose name is on the ballot for a fourth position, and passing judgment on the Physical Plant and Equipment Levy.

For anyone who's been to the polls before, there's nothing tricky about the voting process for the listed candidate or the PPEL referendum. Where we all need to "go to school" is for the write-in ballots. For your vote to count, you will need to know which seats your favorite candidates are running for, how to spell their names, and remember to connect both ends of the arrows that officially cue the election judges to count your votes.

In other words, only well-prepared voters need apply.

Easier to accomplish, but no less important, is voting on the Physical Plant and Equipment Levy, first approved 10 years ago and set to expire next year. In looking at the years 2001 to 2011, the current board made a very conservative estimate of $3.14 million in PPEL needs over the next decade. That's the money required to replace our buses and repair our buildings on a reasonable schedule, buy a very limited amount of educational technology, and ultimately help ensure the health and safety of our students and staff.

We divided the $3.14 million by 10, and came up with an annual figure of $314,000. This is a slight increase from our current PPEL levy (which is not high enough to keep our buses, buildings and equipment in good repair), but because our debt service costs are going down, if the PPEL passes, our overall school-related taxes should stay just about the same.

While I may harbor the heretical hope that most get-out-the-vote campaigns do not succeed, this column is an exception because I trust you to choose well—and everyone else who takes the few minutes required to master the special nuances of this election.

Just about everyone who goes to the polls next Tuesday will, by necessity, have done their homework. That may not make for a huge turnout, but it will result in an informed electorate and, I trust, in wise decisions on election day.

Because only the best-informed will be participating, your vote will mean more than ever to the future of our schools and our community. Please make sure it counts.

TAKING THE FORK IN THE ROAD

This month—to paraphrase baseball legend Yogi Berra—when Mid-Prairie voters came to the fork in the road, they took it.

Even though there were no guarantees about who would be sitting in half the board seats after the election, or who will serve as superintendent next year, our community recognized the September 12 PPEL vote as a turning point in Mid-Prairie's history. A decade ago, the original PPEL squeaked by with a bare majority, and just last year, a proposed Instructional Support Levy was soundly defeated.

As members of the board, we postponed taking this PPEL vote to you until we had done our homework and held public hearings. Even then, we worried about its fate. Had the levy failed, the dollars would have been sorely missed, but the rejection might have been even more devastating to school morale. However, to our collective credit, when our community came to the fork in the road, "we took it"—passing the PPEL by a nearly two-to-one margin.

Your willingness to invest your hard-earned dollars in our schools not only deserves respect, it also demands our redoubled efforts. You've done what we've asked in terms of providing resources to our schools. Now it's up to us to deliver.

While Yogi tried to convince the world he was an intellectual underachiever (when asked, "How did you like school when you were growing up?" he replied, "Closed!"), his words often displayed a sly wisdom. As such, before school supporters celebrate the PPEL outcome for too long, we would do well to remember Berra's admonition, "If you don't know where you are going, you will wind up somewhere else."

Where is Mid-Prairie heading this year? Well, before October is over, we will start work is on hiring a superintendent—and by "we," I literally hope "we."

I'd love to see a full-spectrum search committee. The group would include civic leaders, school employees, students, parents and private individuals. Together, we would define the qualities we want in a superintendent, share our vision with the pool of potential leaders, and select a chief executive from among those who apply.

Your resounding PPEL vote, combined with the superb slate of board candidates this fall, will attract excellent applicants to our top job. The more we can make this search a community effort, the more likely it is we'll select a great superintendent, and the better chance the new CEO will have of understanding of our educational aspirations.

Two other tasks seem paramount. The first is communicating what we're trying to accomplish in our schools, and the second is looking deep within ourselves to make sure we're doing the absolute best job we can with the resources we've been provided.

Too often, public entities only parley with people when they're passing the hat. This year, there won't be another PPEL vote, and I suspect any similar initiatives are some time off. That makes it the perfect time to talk without the perception that we're looking for a handout. It's a chance to spread our message and, more important, to hear yours.

In terms of looking inward, this past year—in compliance with state reporting requirements—we collected reams of data outlining the performance of our students. By carefully sifting the numbers we have, and by collecting data we don't have yet, we can better assess the strengths and weaknesses of our educational endeavors.

The self-study process is critical to our district's ongoing improvement. However, for us to adequately evaluate whether we're doing the job the public deserves, it is imperative the public join in that judgment. If you're interested in helping shape our schools and don't hear your telephone ring, call us. I promise you, we'll listen.

Yogi Berra famously noted, "You can observe a lot just by watching." We watched the votes come in last week, and saw the commitment you made to our future.

Now it's your turn to watch us, or better yet, join us as we travel beyond the fork in Mid-Prairie's road. Like all of life, it's sure to be an adventure. As Yogi once told Phil Rizzuto, when his fellow Yankee feared they were lost, "Yeah, but we're making great time!"

CIVICS—AND CIVILITY

The first time I saw politicians at work in Iowa, they were Minnesotans! And, I'm sad to say, it's gone downhill ever since.

Hubert Humphrey and Eugene McCarthy were running for president, and I was a juvenile political junkie looking for action. While Minnesota's "twins" were interested in voters three times my age, I emerged from my adventure with two autographs, a hearty handshake from the "Happy Warrior," and even an elevator ride with "Clean Gene."

Even though our nation was not in a good mood that year—Vietnam, assassinations and riots were among 1968's contributions to history—on that day, through 7-year-old eyes, these men were kind and decent leaders.

Civility doesn't come so easily these days. While tight budgets give politicians reason to be grumpy, no reasonable person can argue the stakes today are higher than 34 years ago. Nonetheless, today's politics seem just plain nasty, and unfortunately, it may be our kids who pay the price for our pouting.

Take Phil Wise, the Legislature's "loudest mouth" for education (take that characterization as you will). I agree with Representative Wise on most issues, but I doubt he wins us many friends when he writes, "Your legislative leaders . . . have become mere bean counters, completely devoid of vision."

If his goal is to increase school funding, why would he—especially as a minority-party member—aggressively offend those whose votes he requires? Seems like bad manners, and poor politics, to me.

Later, after failing to shift money from roads to education, Wise wrote: "I chose kids over concrete. . . . A majority of the Iowa House did not share my . . . values. . . .

"If a few road projects get delayed a year, that is better than Iowa children loosing (sic) a year of educational opportunity. That road building can be made up. A child loosing a full year of intellectual growth may not be something that can be made up."

(Note: If politicians claiming ethical and intellectual superiority have a "loose" mastery of written English, it might be "Wise" for them to descend from their pedestals before deriding their colleagues.)

Sadly, Wise may be right about our kids—but no one cares to listen. The same was true for legislative leaders from both parties who spoke to a January conference of the Iowa Association of School Boards.

The legislators counseled us not to seek a 4 percent increase in allowable growth—because given Iowa's income, it wasn't going to happen. So, what occurred after the last legislator left the room? Our lobbyists enjoined us to march en masse to the capitol to seek a 4 percent increase.

If I were a legislator, would I listen to us? Why should I, if we lacked the courtesy to listen to them?

While a last-minute deal may scuttle these numbers (I hope), the net impact of our lobbying appears negligible at best, and negative at worst. We got 1 percent in allowable growth, but a third of the actual dollars are being pulled from our own pockets. Moreover, while allowable growth inched forward, other funding fell back, so we ended about where we started, except more isolated and irate.

Humphrey, history's Happy Warrior, said, "To err is human. To blame someone else is politics." He's still right. Too often, we'd rather fix the blame than the problem.

In a more tragic dispute, sociologist Amitai Etzioni recently wrote about the Palestinian-Israeli conflict, "Progress toward ending the violence, it is presumed, will come once the party in the wrong yields. But what makes this conflict so bitter is that it is not a clash between right and wrong, but between two rights."

School funding is also a fight between two rights—educational responsibility and economic reality. As Etzioni concluded, "Therein lies a possible solution, if we can get past the myths and begin gradually to find points of commonality and compromise."

Commonality and compromise also require another "c" word—communication, which is where we need some work.

Not over in the Middle East, but right here in the Middle West.

A MAD, MAD WORLD

This evening, I took a walk past Kalona Elementary. Peering into the empty playground, I saw a stray soccer ball littering the landscape. The playground, the quiet, and the excess wealth represented by the forgotten ball reminded me of—Afghanistan.

"You left your soccer ball?" I can imagine an incredulous Kalona father asking. "Don't you know there are kids in this world who would kill to have their own soccer ball?"

Unfortunately for Dad, and the world, that statement is truer than many of us might think.

Afghanistan was on my mind as the result of an e-mail I received earlier today. Forwarded several times, it started with a photographer responding to a class of 4th graders wondering what it's like to work in the Afghan war zone.

One boy asks, "Do most boys walk around carrying guns?"

The woman answers, "No, there are a handful of boys that have Kalashnikov rifles, and it is frightening to be around someone really young that might not be trained properly, but on the whole most boys run and play, unarmed, like most kids in the U.S."

(Maybe I'm just twitchy, but any "really young" person packing a Kalashnikov makes me nervous, even if he is "trained properly." And what exactly does she mean by "most kids"?)

Later, the class asks if 10-year-old girls, previously banned by the Taliban from attending school, can read the signs in town.

The photographer answers, "Well, you probably heard that girls were banned from going to school for five years. If they were caught studying their fathers were beaten and sometimes killed, but even so many women risked their lives and had secret schools for girls that would meet at different times daily for fear of getting caught. . . .

"The people who live in areas destroyed by bombs have less money and resources, and their girls are not as well-schooled . . . but on the whole the girls are REALLY excited about going back to school. The problem is that there are girls who are 14 in classes with boys that are nine."

(Not that the boys are complaining.)

President Bush planned a trip to Afghanistan to welcome 1.4 million Afghan kids back to class this spring, much as Mid-Prairie's "greeters" do each morning at our schools. Downplaying politics, the president extended his *No Child Left Behind* agenda to the international arena.

"This past weekend, many young girls for the first time in their life went to school," Bush said. "It's important for the young in America to understand we went in not as conquerors, but as liberators."

Underscoring the profound differences between our societies, though, the Afghan pupils made it to their classes, but the American president did not. Bush had asked Oprah Winfrey to join him, but when she backed out ("Given her responsibility to the show, she isn't adding anything to her calendar," said her PR rep), he put his visit on hold until, as the *Chicago Tribune* reported, his staff could find "another celebrity who shares her credibility and popularity."

(Remind me: Who is rescuing whom from the madmen—and women?)

When our American entourage ultimately arrives in Afghanistan, I hope we share with the Afghan students our notions about free speech, the dignity of women, and even put in a plug for religious and ethnic tolerance.

I also hope, though, we have the humility to learn from what our hosts have to teach us. Listen to what the photographer told the 4th graders about Afghanistan's most recent disaster.

"I just covered an earthquake that killed hundreds of people and destroyed thousands of homes, and when I was photographing the rubble people who had absolutely nothing were inviting me in for tea, and the little girls were bringing me flowers. The Afghans are so resilient and strong. I hope to be more like them when I get home."

As a father, I get frustrated when I see athletic equipment lying forgotten in a playground. But when I think of the kids who'd kill for a ball like the one I saw tonight, I thank heaven for my upscale annoyances—and hope our incredibly fortunate society remembers to do the same.

Chapter Nine

Achievement

DUST AND SWEAT AND BLOOD

If you like sumo wrestling, you'd have loved the last board meeting. Voices were raised, arms were waved and tables were pounded.

Board members and administrators fought over what value (if any) our recent report to the Iowa Department of Education had, grappled over the proper role (if any) of standardized tests in evaluating our performance, and clashed over creating a school improvement plan that actually had a chance of enhancing our schools.

In short, it was the best meeting of my 13 months on the board—and, according to the surprising results of the recent Iowa Association of School Boards' "Lighthouse Study," typical of what might be expected from "high-achieving school districts."

That night's "deliberations" resulted in four goals for this academic year: developing a school improvement plan, conducting a search for a superintendent, funding all-day everyday kindergarten, and prioritizing expenditures from the Physical Plant and Equipment Levy.

While each goal is important, it was the passion with which we arrived at them that gave me so much hope. According to the IASB, in successful districts the "specific attitudes" of key players were "remarkably different, but in all cases the people interviewed appeared to care deeply about doing the right thing for children."

The Lighthouse Study reports all great districts share two characteristics—they never excuse failure, and they expect all children to succeed.

"In the low-achieving districts, the board/superintendent team and school personnel . . . tended to view students as limited by characteristics such as their income or home situation, and accepted schools as they were. Their focus was on managing the school environment, rather than changing or improving it." Ouch.

The study makes it clear school boards must do more to create cultures in which education thrives. According to IASB Executive Director Ron Rice, "We used to think that if you hired a good superintendent then you should let them do their work, but we're beginning to rethink that." He adds "We went in thinking it wouldn't make any difference, but in fact, what school board members know about the curriculum and their belief systems have everything to do with student outcomes."

Astoundingly, while "impertinence" is an unexpected value upheld by the IASB, "impatience" is another! The IASB says "stuck" school districts expected to "take years to see any improvements," while "moving" districts expected "improvements in student achievement quickly as a result of initiatives."

That's what makes our session, with all its hooting and hollering, so hopeful. The enthusiasm with which arguments were advanced that evening speaks to an environment in which our shared educational visions can become realities.

Oscar Wilde once said, "I dislike arguments of any kind. They are always vulgar, and often convincing." Because of our willingness to forcefully address the issues we face, I am convinced that by the end of this year, we can create a School Improvement Plan that will far exceed the minimal requirements of the Department of Education, hire a great superintendent, get all-day everyday kindergarten off the ground, and put our PPEL spending plan in order—and most important, improve the lives of every one of our students.

It may seem like a tall order, but in the words of Teddy Roosevelt, another fan of a good argument, "The credit belongs to the man who is actively in the arena, whose face is marred by the dust and sweat and blood; who strives valiantly; who errs and comes short again and again . . . who at the best, knows in the end the triumph of high achievement, and who, at worst, if he fails, at least fails while doing greatly."

Whether you choose to watch from ringside or actively join in our "discussion," this is one match you don't want to miss. The best thing about it is that in the educational arena, like few others, everyone involved has the chance to come out a winner.

HARD JOB. NO PAY. INTERESTED?

As I sit down to write this column, I am 15 minutes removed from mowing my lawn. Even though it's a dirty, sweaty, noisy job, I love cutting the grass. Unlike many things I do, when I am done mowing, I can tell I've accomplished something.

In a couple weeks, you'll have the same chance to do some hard work that's worth doing. No, I'm not asking you to mow my yard. Instead, I'm asking you to consider taking out nomination papers to run for the school board.

This fall, there will be four positions on the ballot. Having spent nearly one year on the board, I now know what the job means in terms of time and energy, but like my colleagues, including those up for reelection, I also have come to appreciate the feeling of satisfaction that comes from having made a difference.

While the final numbers aren't in, this year we succeeded in building up our bank account by tens of thousands of dollars, and are making excellent progress toward achieving our goal of "five percent in five years" for the undesignated, unspent balance.

We were also able to begin all-day everyday kindergarten for a handful of children identified as being especially able to benefit from the opportunity. The positive reaction of the parents, combined with the evidence that early educational success makes a huge difference in long-term learning, is pushing the board to press for all-day everyday kindergarten for every child. While I'm just one vote, my guess is next year will be the last for "All day, every-OTHER-day kindergarten" in the district.

We've also succeeded in using a $32,000 federal grant for a *Class Size Reduction Project* that has paid clear dividends, although it's only been in place less than half the school year. At Washington Township, for example, students in 1st grade made six-tenths of a grade's progress in reading since the start of the new year. In 2nd grade, they made eight-tenths of a year's advance in a half-year's time. In 3rd grade, the increase was a stunning 1.1 grades, literally more than doubling the learning that might be predicted from the calendar alone.

I'm not going to lie. Should you run, you'll have your share of challenges. We'll start your term by reacting to the fate of the Physical Plant and Equipment Levy, which will be on the same ballot as the school board election. No matter which way that vote goes, we'll be making decisions based upon its outcome that will affect education in the district for years to come.

We'll also be selecting a new superintendent. While the school board sets policy for the district, the superintendent sets the tone for every Mid-Prairie classroom. A more important decision may not be made this decade.

I know you're busy, but so is everyone. The question you should ask yourself is not, "Do I have time?" but rather, "What am I doing that's more important?"

A recent book titled *Bowling Alone* describes how our culture has changed in our lifetimes. When I was a child, people bowled in leagues. Now that I'm an adult, people bowl as much as ever, but instead of joining teams, we almost all "bowl alone."

According to the author, Robert D. Putnam, "These and other changes in American society have meant that fewer and fewer of us find that the League of Women Voters, or the United Way, or the Shriners, or the monthly bridge club, or even a Sunday picnic with friends fits the way we have come to live. Our growing social-capital deficit threatens educational performance, safe neighborhoods, equitable tax collection, democratic responsiveness, everyday honesty, and even our health and happiness."

We are lucky enough to live in communities where people know their neighbors and where, just as fortunately, it doesn't cost a fortune to become involved in public service. Last year, my election expenses included a passport photo taken for the papers, a drive to the candidates' forum, and turning in typewritten answers to questions posed by the media. The total cost of my "campaign"? Probably less than $10.

Yes, serving on the school board is sometimes a dirty, sweaty, noisy job—and the pay is not only lousy, it's nonexistent. Still, every once in a while you can tell you've accomplished something—not only for yourself, but for your community, for today and for tomorrow. I hope you'll consider applying for the job.

COACH. POLITICIAN. ENTREPRENEUR. ICON.

The search for a new superintendent for the Mid-Prairie Community School District has begun. For our efforts to be successful, we must first decide upon what we want in a chief executive.

Most superintendents' job descriptions list the following requirements—teaching and administrative credentials, and successful classroom, supervisory and budgetary experience. To be honest, any search
committee concentrating on these qualities will probably hire the
bureaucrat it deserves.

While none of these attributes is a bad thing, they ignore the real job of
modern superintendents—creating communities where parents, staff and
citizens enthusiastically embrace education, and in which student learning
can thrive.

How do you find such superintendents? First, forget about the official job duties. Instead, look at the other roles outstanding leaders must
assume.

Head coach. From Day One, everyone must know who's in charge. Phil
Jackson, the best basketball coach in a generation, propelled a Los Angeles Lakers team that had consistently fallen short of its potential into the
NBA finals during his first year at the helm. His players knew if they were
going to be champions, they needed to listen to—and act upon—what their
coach had to say. His results speak for themselves.

Unlike some bosses, Jackson doesn't browbeat his players into obedience.
Instead, he manages to both teach his team the triangle offense and explore
treatises such as George Bernard Shaw's *Man and Superman*. According to
Jackson, "It's a trust sequence. If you keep trusting people more and more,
they get into it."

Shaquille O'Neal's take on Jackson? "It's Phil's job to inspire us, but it
gets translated down to me," says O'Neal. "It was Aristotle who said excellence is not a singular act but a habit. You are what you repeatedly do."
There couldn't be a more perfect statement to describe the role of a great
superintendent.

Politician. Most superintendents never see their name on an election ballot, but the best ones go before the voters literally every day. They're out
pressing the flesh, getting community leaders, parents and kids excited about
education. Like skilled politicians, successful superintendents forge ironclad
relationships with their constituents, and create the coalitions required to
move public policy in their direction.

Every time a superintendent goes to a basketball game, it's a campaign
appearance, and every time one talks with a parent or teacher, it's a campaign speech. The job of all school supporters is to tell the truth, again and

again, until everyone hears the message and understands. If we've done our job, election day is one like almost any other, and we won't need to worry about what the voters decide.

Entrepreneur. The days of erecting schools and watching kids stream through the doors are coming to a screeching halt. Already, Iowa's open enrollment laws have begun to impose the discipline of the market upon the industry. For each child from a neighboring district we persuade to "buy our product," that means $4,500—each year—for our schools.

A family with three children, over 13-year academic careers, represents a gain, or loss, of more than $175,000 in current dollars to Mid-Prairie. With that much money at stake, it's incumbent upon superintendents to channel resources to our best programs and, like an entrepreneur with a bottom line to defend, curtail those efforts no longer carrying their fair share of the load.

Cultural icon. I'm not talking about Elvis Presley or Marilyn Monroe. Instead, I'm talking about leaders like Bill Gates and Martin Luther King who—by the force of their words, deeds and powerful personalities—created cultures that every person in their respective organizations understood deep into their bones.

Anyone who challenged Microsoft or the Southern Christian Leadership Conference knew they were going up against the best. The cultures they created not only transformed their organizations, but the societies in which they lived. The same responsibility, and potential, awaits the individual we hire as superintendent.

Head coach. Politician. Entrepreneur. Cultural icon. The job of a modern superintendent is both an impossible challenge and an unparalleled opportunity. My hope is we get someone competent, confident—and perhaps even crazy—enough to take it on.

DON'T KICK THE BALL ON THE ROOF

Ralph Waldo Emerson wrote, "The secret in education lies in respecting the student." Like most maxims, it's filled with good intentions, but is too seldom acted upon—except, I'm pleased to report, in our current superintendent search.

During its canvass of the various Mid-Prairie constituents, the Iowa Association of School Boards held interviews with 31 of our most important stakeholders, our students. What they said might surprise you, not because of their unique perspectives, which you might expect, but for their wisdom, which I—in my prejudice—did not.

While hardly old enough to have a historical perspective, the students hit it on the head in describing our region as "a nice place to be with lots of friendly people," and themselves as the latest in long lines of "many generations of relatives."

Our elementary students list our strengths as our teachers, buildings, activities, library, "Pretend Time," lunches, music, physical education and recess, items I expected to see. What I didn't anticipate was them taking special note of the efforts to raise money for playground equipment, the Nature Center and our community potlucks.

Our high schoolers listed sports, band, drama, Future Farmers of America, student council, West Campus, supportive teachers and block scheduling as strong points. They also noted the diversity in courses, competition for grades, the physical plant, a smooth-running administration, collegial staff members and safe schools (something I wouldn't have thought to mention a generation ago).

In terms of weaknesses, our Golden Hawks paid special attention to school culture. They said everyone needs to do "a better job of supporting the school," and that there should be a reduction in "the tension between Kalona and Wellman." They also suggested, however, the "problem appears to be with the parents more than the students."

In terms of curriculum, they wanted more courses overall and especially more Advanced Placement classes. They suggested "we should not only look at what students are learning, but make use of different methods to teach how students learn."

Perhaps most impressive was the call for the new superintendent to "Challenge all students to succeed," and to "See to it that all teachers have high expectations of their students. Some teachers are really lenient. We need more challenging classes."

When it came to weaknesses, our younger students nobly looked to themselves first. They said "all the kids need to play better during recess," "need to treat the bathroom better," and (my personal favorite) "don't kick the basketball on the roof."

The students also listed the personal qualities they're seeking in the new CEO. High schoolers want someone who is accessible, open-minded,

creative, passionate, and willing to "stand by their beliefs." Toward that
end, the superintendent should be willing to "sit down with the student
council," and be a "natural leader" and "go getter."

Similarly, our grade schoolers want someone who is "nice," "makes the
school look tidy," hires more teachers and helps the teachers in their work.
They also want someone who is "smart and makes good rules," "has a
sense of humor," is "honest and fair," and (most important) "likes kids"
and (most surprising) "likes animals."

The pre-teens say the superintendent should be "willing to visit our
schools . . . and take an interest in our activities." The new boss should also
be "able to take a joke," not be "boring," and (thankfully) can be "either a
boy or a girl."

Emerson also wrote, "I pay the schoolmaster, but it is the school-
boys who educate my son." Our students have compiled an impressive
list of superintendent qualifications. I hope we have the good sense to
pay attention.

NO TASK, RIGHTLY DONE, IS TRULY PRIVATE

Others may have different opinions (and probably do, as you'll see), but
for me, the most telling moment of our just-completed superintendent
search occurred during a public interview with the board. After handling
25 of our toughest questions, one finalist tossed a softball in return:
"Which of your hiring criteria do you think is most important?"

This question came after hundreds of collective hours spent in public meetings refining our combined thoughts, and many more hours
spent privately pondering the qualities we sought in our new superintendent.

After all that ruminating, you'd think our answers would be reflexive,
or that they would at least resemble one another's—but my recollection is
that our seven board members championed at least that many answers,
even though there were only six criteria from which to choose. Such is the
glory of democracy.

It's in that spirit of intellectual diversity that we welcome Mark Schneider
in his soon-to-be role of superintendent. Although "Mr. Schneider's" Mid-
Prairie experience dates from an era when electric typewriters ruled the

Earth, Mark would probably be the first to tell you the challenges facing modern superintendents are many. Consider this condensed version of the criteria the board used to guide our hiring process:

We wanted someone who could create a culture in which exceptional academic and professional performance are encouraged, expected and evaluated on an ongoing basis—and who could put forward formal processes to achieve those ends.

We wanted someone who would appreciate the special qualities of our district, and who could integrate our community into our decision-making.

We wanted someone with superb speaking, writing and listening skills, and who could provide concrete examples of effective communications with his or her students, staff, community and board members.

We wanted someone with successful leadership experience, who encouraged innovation, and who would channel individual efforts toward our common goals.

We wanted someone who could prudently manage our fiscal resources, who could explain how buildings and grounds should be maintained, and who could minutely describe their preferred process for requisitions.

We wanted someone who not only believed "All students can learn," but who had the courage to define sensitive terms such as *educational accountability* in public.

In short, we wanted someone faster than a speeding bullet and capable of leaping tall buildings in a single bound (and X-ray vision wouldn't hurt either).

As it turns out, we selected someone who actually might have an "S" monogrammed on his shirt, but as with all school districts, Mid-Prairie's strength will never reside in one individual, but in its many supporters' combined efforts and abilities. Like the mythical Superman, if we all pull together, we can no doubt move mountains.

A college president turned U.S. president, Woodrow Wilson, once said, "No task, rightly done, is truly private. It is part of the world's work." Through our superintendent search, we not only learned about our applicants, but about ourselves. That wisdom is our real power.

We are about to enter a new era in the history of our district, with an experienced Mid-Prairie hand at our helm. Now that we've selected our skipper, it's all hands on deck. If we all row in roughly the same direction, we're in for a great ride.

"FAILING" TO LEARN

Human babies are learning miracles. In a few short years, they evolve from the most helpless creatures in nature to self-directed little people capable of walking, talking and even tying their own shoelaces—a task mastered by no other species on this planet.

What makes babies "whiz kids"? In short, infants gleefully embrace failure. Learning to walk, they take a step, fall flat, laugh, pull themselves up and try again. When their coordination and confidence finally kick in, they're off to the races.

With reckless abandon, they keep soaking in smarts and skills until we start "correcting" their errors, whether through smiley faces and red checkmarks, or actual smiles and frowns. Being master learners, children are soon socialized into seeking perfection.

By adulthood, they learn their best bet is to avoid tasks at which they might fail. The older I get, the more I'm convinced it's the fear of failing— or of exposing our ignorance—that makes us grown-ups as dense and dull as we tend to be.

While it's easy to talk up the rewards of risk, few volunteer to be the fair-haired child for fiasco. That's why I'm proud that throughout Mid-Prairie, we're demonstrating our willingness to take reasonable risks—and thrilled some bets are paying off. Among the more prominent examples:

Block scheduling. When it might have been safer to stick with the status quo, a board before my time had the courage adopt this less-conventional schedule. That decision allowed Mid-Prairie High School to implement its trailblazing Adviser-Advisee Program, which in turn enabled MPHS to earn the FINE (First in the Nation in Education) Award this spring. Out of Iowa's 371 school districts, and perhaps half again as many high schools, MPHS was the only high school to win a FINE Award this year.

Grantsmanship. W. C. Fields once said, "If at first you don't succeed, try, try again. Then quit. There's no point in being a [darn] fool about it." This spring, our administrators proved the late, great comedian dead wrong.

After two unsuccessful attempts to secure support for a geothermal heating system at Kalona Elementary, our administrative team didn't quit. They tried a third time, landing a $95,000 grant. Not only did our administrators come up winners, so did our district, our taxpayers and our students.

There are numerous other examples in which Mid-Prairie has made well-considered, yet "risky," decisions: passing a PPEL to support our physical plant and equipment needs, instituting all-day everyday kindergarten, implementing interest-based bargaining, choosing a geothermal heating system over a conventional furnace, and in perhaps the most under-recognized development this year, committing ourselves to a seven-year curriculum renewal cycle in a time of uncertain funding.

I hope all our decisions work out, but if we can't tolerate occasional failure, we have no right to expect extraordinary success—which is, I hope, the aspiration we have not only for our students, but for our district and ourselves.

Fortunately, failure is starting to earn the respect it deserves, as exemplified in a recent *Des Moines Register* headline—*Expect to Fail, Graduates Told.*

Former Labor Secretary Robert Reich, my favorite Clinton administration official, told Grinnell College graduates that "self-knowledge comes from failing . . . and have no doubts about it. You will fail in some way at some time."

Reich told of being fired from some jobs, and of spending too much time in others at the expense of his family. He counseled against safe, unfulfilling careers—and encouraged the graduates not to evade their inevitable failures, but to learn from them.

Like Grinnell's, Mid-Prairie's Class of 2002 is taking its first steps out in the "real world." As long as our graduates don't forget what they knew as babies—keep falling, laughing and getting up until you get it right—they should do just fine.

CHANCE ENCOUNTERS OF THE EDUCATIONAL KIND

It might not sound exciting to you, but the best experience I've had as a board member came at the local library. As I scanned *Sports Illustrated*, a more cultured woman approached me and asked if I had seen Mid-Prairie High School's Annual Report, which was also available on the periodical rack.

She told me how the report was stuffed with tables and graphs telling the MPHS story. In reply, I probably said something like, "*Sports Illustrated*? I thought this was *Smithsonian*," and slunk off, chastened by this erudite citizen.

Truth be told, the *MPHS Annual Report* is truly a treasure. You'll find everything from attendance rates to graduate surveys, and if you're like me, you'll feel smarter when you're finished reading than when you got started.

Take our ACT scores (disclosure: I work for ACT). Mid-Prairie examinees earned average composite scores of 22.3 last year, a point better than the national average, and 1.5 points better than our scores from 1988. Moreover, while M-P scored a point below Iowa's average in 1988, we've not only caught our statewide peers, we've outpaced them three out of the past five years.

While keeping relative scores can be important, education is about self-improvement. Again, the numbers are illuminating. In 1988, M-P's math scores were three points below our reading scores. Somebody obviously went to work. Last year, math actually led M-P's pack, and the spread between our highest and lowest scoring curricular areas plunged to 0.8 points, or one-fourth the gap of 13 years ago.

Other numbers that jump from the pages: the 33 percent increase in credits required for graduation, our 95.6 percent attendance rate, the decrease in annual in-school suspensions from 73 to 31 since 1996, and in out-of-school suspensions from 31 to 1 (yes, one) over the same period.

Twenty new courses have been added to our curriculum in the last four years, including Local Area Network Design, Personal Finance, and four Advanced Placement courses (Biology, Calculus, Chemistry and History). In 1998, Mid-Prairie's total "AP" enrollment was 12. By this year, that number had skyrocketed to 84.

Of course, some folks aren't fans of statistics (their motto, stolen from a bumper sticker: *Give Me Ambiguity, or Give Me Something Else*). For them, activities to enhance school climate may tell the story: food drives, staff appreciation days, birthday cards for all students, fundraisers to fight leukemia and cystic fibrosis, leaf-raking for the elderly, and elementary student mentoring.

Next month, many of us will be sharing Mid-Prairie's story with teams from the Iowa Department of Education and the North Central Association as part of their evaluation processes. From my perspective, the MPHS Annual Report and similar documents from across our district tell a compelling story about where we are and the direction we're heading.

While I have no elementary or secondary accreditation experience, a decade ago I had the "opportunity" to direct my college's self-study in

Valdez, Alaska. To my astonishment, our report and subsequent visit weren't burdens, but chances to explain the good work we were doing—and to receive pointers on how we might do even better.

And, as at the Kalona Library, it was a chance encounter I most remember.

Valdez is literally 110 miles from the next wide spot in the road, so we noticed visitors.

When the evaluators arrived and waited for their luggage at our airport, a member of our college council didn't recognize the man standing next to him (everyone knows EVERYONE in Valdez), deduced he was an evaluator, and proceeded to bend his ear about our school, our self-study, and about how pleased they would be with their visit.

The evaluator was stunned a marine terminal worker knew so much about our college, much less our accreditation report, but such understanding and enthusiasm spoke to him like printed paper never could.

The next time you're in our libraries, ask for Mid-Prairie's reports. You may not have a chance encounter with a visiting evaluator, but the truth is, you're our permanent evaluation team. Your informed and enthusiastic input will help us make the most of our most valuable resource—Mid-Prairie's children.

YOU *GUTSE* ENOUGH?

If there is a Holy Grail in science, it is the *Grand Unified Theory*. This hypothesis would combine space, time and mass into a single conceptual framework. Physicists have yet to find the *GUT,* and it may be out of the reach of mortals to do so, but they haven't given up on assembling the universe into one rational arrangement.

In education, the goals are less lofty—but in this case, a *Grand Unified Theory of School Evaluation* (or *GUTSE*) may also be more achievable. This year the most important issue facing Iowa education—according to Governor Vilsack, and the legislative leadership—will be finding a formula that allows Iowa to pay its teachers more, while at the same time tying the compensation to classroom performance.

Two blue-ribbon panels recently released reports addressing Iowa's impending teacher shortage. The *Business Forum* and the *Forsyth Commission*

provided ample evidence that because of Iowa's sliding teacher compensation, both the quality and quantity of our educators could plummet in the
decade ahead.

In their recommendations, the groups attempted to change the prevailing pay paradigm in which teachers get more money merely by racking up
more years' experience and educational credits. As the groups noted,
whether today's students are learning any more in exchange for that
higher pay is, quite seriously, beside the point.

The hard part about squaring this circle is that many bargaining groups
oppose linking pay to performance, arguing such schemes overemphasize
test scores and underestimate the "art" of teaching. At the same time,
many legislators insist they won't come up with another "quid" without a
commensurate "pro quo."

That's where a *GUTSE* approach comes in. Instead of having one
day's tests determine a teacher's paycheck, which is inappropriate, I
suggest five measures—1) peer evaluations, 2) administrative evaluations, 3) weighted workloads, 4) student and/or parent evaluations, and
5) standardized test scores. Educators without obvious links to test
scores (e.g., art, music and physical education teachers) could have four
evaluation criteria rather than five.

Peer evaluations—the system for which teachers could devise themselves—would be immune from "grade inflation" by using standard deviations to compare individual performance, a fancy term for grading on the
curve. The same would be true for the administrative and student/parent
evaluations.

Enrollment could be weighted by class preparations or the presence of
special needs children, but would recognize that teachers with 25 students
have different workloads than those with 15. Test scores would measure
this year's progress, so today's great teacher isn't saddled with low scores
caused by last year's underachiever.

Pay increases would be targeted to teachers who make the most difference,
using the standard deviation as a multiplier. For example, if 4 percent more
money is available for raises, an "average" teacher would get a 4 percent raise,
a good teacher (one-half deviation above the mean) would get 6 percent, and
a mediocre teacher (one-half deviation below) would get 2 percent.

A great teacher (two deviations above) would get 12 percent, and a terrible teacher (two deviations below) would see a pay cut of 4 percent—

something almost impossible to achieve today. Remember though, no matter how you slice the pay in this example, the overall pie would be 4 percent bigger. It's the slices of the pie that get bigger and smaller, depending upon how each teacher grades out.

Most evaluation criteria would be based upon formal School Improvement Goals, increasing the incentive to achieve those goals (and providing an obvious framework for professional development). Administrators would be subject to the same scrutiny. They can just as easily be judged on these criteria as teachers (and by teachers), and aggregated test scores and enrollment figures could also feed into their performance measures.

The "grand and unified" part of *GUTSE* would come from public participation in the form of a 10 percent overlay to the calculations described above. A statistically valid sample of the public would be surveyed to assess their satisfaction with our schools.

A unanimous positive evaluation would boost the 4 percent average increase by the maximum one-tenth, to 4.4 percent (the state would probably be pleased to fund the 0.4 percent extra raise). A unanimously negative evaluation would drop the 4 percent overall increase by one-tenth to 3.6 percent (the remaining 0.4 percent would be plowed into professional development to improve next year's performance).

I wouldn't worry about public participation. When people suspect their answers are going into a vertical file, never to see the light of day, their survey forms are much more likely to go into the circular file. When they know their answers will truly affect what happens in our schools, they'll answer.

Similarly, staff who know their paychecks will depend, in part, upon public input will be more likely to put their teaching skills to work to build broad-based public support for their schools. That should be happening today, but too often isn't.

Nonteaching staff, such as bus drivers, cooks and custodians, could also participate in the evaluation plan. Their efforts make a huge, but under-appreciated, contribution to the success of our schools; a *GUTSE* approach would remedy that failing. Finally, while our school board members aren't paid, survey results would also serve as legitimate district and board grades, measurements that are never made in the current system outside thumbs-up or thumbs-down elections.

This universal feedback loop puts every public servant in the same boat. That creates incentives for everyone to row in the same direction—toward a Promised Land of demonstrably excellent teaching and enhanced student performance, and toward greater public support for our schools.

The legislature and the governor "want" to pay teachers more, but must find a politically acceptable means of doing so. This plan provides that mechanism. For example, in exchange for a 10 percent boost in support, the state could demand that districts agree to a *GUTSE* approach.

That way, instead of throwing more coins down a wishing well and hoping for performance (our current approach), we would see real results, as assessed by professional educators, the students sitting in our classrooms, the parents who send their kids to school, and the people who pay the bills, Iowa's taxpayers.

Is this *GUTSE*? Big time. But if teachers want the public to pay them more, they should be able to prove they're worth it. They can make a good case now, but were we to adopt a *Grand Unified Theory of School Evaluation,* they could make a great case.

Let's see if our political leaders and our educational establishment have the intestinal fortitude to make it happen.

UNCLE SAM NEEDS ASSISTANCE

Iowa identified 26 schools this month as "needing assistance" under the federal *No Child Left Behind Act.* The schools must now offer to bus affected students to other schools within their districts, and provide tutoring and other services.

It was an ID Iowa made under duress.

"This is a federal definition," complained Kathi Slaughter of the Department of Education to the *Des Moines Register.* "We don't use test scores to label schools."

Uhhh . . . but that's exactly what they did. And, as a person who's employed by the testing industry, I'm here to say (as a private individual) that using test scores as the sole criterion to identify schools as "failures" is educational malpractice.

If you don't like my definition of *malpractice,* ask someone who knows—a lawyer.

"There is no magic to any particular test score," writes Arthur Coleman, formerly of the U.S. Office of Civil Rights. "Psychometric standards confirm that a single test score should not be used as the sole criterion to make high-stakes educational decisions affecting students."

Lest you think Coleman is an anti-testing activist, I learned of his work when he spoke at last year's ACT annual meeting. Rather than advocating either extreme in the testing debate, Coleman suggests four criteria for evaluating high-stakes tests.

First, what justifies a test? Coleman argues that BEFORE you give a test, know why you're giving it. "Conclusions one may draw from the results are meaningless," he writes, "absent clear test objectives." Given that *No Child Left Behind* wasn't passed until AFTER the tests in question were given, it seems a stretch to suggest the law meets that standard.

Coleman's second principle: Is there alignment between what's tested and what's taught? Iowa, alone among the 50 states, doesn't have a state curriculum, leaving that to local boards. In the absence of a single curriculum, it's hard to imagine a single test that can generate the results the feds are after.

Question three: How are the tests interpreted? Coleman says decision-makers must consider "academic factors in addition to the test scores that may affirm or challenge the high stakes conclusions." In other words, "Educators, don't be afraid to do your jobs. Don't let one test score override everything else you know about a student."

Coleman's final question: "What evidence exists regarding the adverse impact of high-stakes decision-making upon discrete groups of students?" That's a fancy way to say if some kids (e.g., free-lunch, rural, female) consistently perform poorly, the school must look as hard at itself as it does at its students.

That's where I shift my concern from the misuse of the tests to the misdirection of the districts. Des Moines Superintendent Eric Witherspoon complained, for example, high-poverty schools were singled out. "If you are a district with affluent students, you are not being sanctioned," he told the *Register*. "I'm very disappointed the only schools being sanctioned have a high percentage of low-income students."

Judy Jeffrey, a state official, added sanctioning schools whose students are failing is a "different philosophy than what the state has held for many, many years."

Maybe I'm just slow, but "sanctioning schools whose students are failing" doesn't seem out of line—especially given the "penalties" prescribed under the law. The parents can send their kids to another school in the same district (which means the district keeps its funding), and the students receive tutoring and other interventions.

In short, some schools seem more afraid of being labeled as "needing assistance" than enthusiastic about providing assistance, which may be why the law was passed in the first place.

Progress is being made. Prairie View School was identified as "needing assistance" in reading. To improve performance, it reassigned teachers at its three elementary schools, and added extended-day programs and summer school.

Guess what—it worked! Students performing below expectations fell from 40 percent a year ago to 23 percent this year. But guess what else? The educational bureaucracy apparently moves more slowly than the allegedly sluggish schools they're evaluating, so the 17-point gain won't count until next year. In short, even when a school turns in a spectacular performance under the feds' strained standards, it takes Uncle Sam 12 months to tally the score.

It's just one test, but it appears some government gurus are "needing assistance."

Chapter Ten

Culture

ADAM WEST HIGH SCHOOL

I've been attending Mid-Prairie board meetings since 1999, but my first school board meeting dates from 1977. I was a senior at Iowa City West High School, and like many seniors, I perhaps had too much time on my hands. You be the judge.

My friends and I thought about our peer institutions—*Cedar Rapids Washington* and *Jefferson*, *Des Moines Lincoln* and *Roosevelt*. While their names weren't exactly cool, they were better than our moniker—*West*, a point on the compass, which in its literal sense defined us not by who we were, but by where we were relative to something else. Pathetic.

So, we went to our school board with a modest proposal—"How about changing our name?" For their convenience, we offered suggestions. To honor local academia, we proposed James Van Allen, discoverer of the Van Allen Radiation Belts.

Our other nominees were Henry David Thoreau, in keeping with West's then-pastoral setting, and Mahatma Gandhi. You gotta think big.

The board members, being adults, were unmoved. They couched their rejection by saying it would cost too much to change the school's stationery, diplomas and the sign out front.

Then, some students came up with the brilliant idea of naming our school after someone already named *West*—for example, author Nathaniel West, actress Mae West, or (my favorite) actor Adam West (you know him as *Batman*).

Again, we didn't get far, but our ultimately academic exercise succeeded in making a serious point: the way we describe ourselves helps shape who we are.

Mid-Prairie's high school and middle school are named after the district. It may be creeping adulthood, but that works fine for me. Just saying *Mid-Prairie* 10 times a day helps instill a subliminal sense of district unity.

On the other hand, our elementary schools are named for their locations. While it's good to have pride in where we come from, it would be nice if in addition to celebrating our geography, we could also project a sense of what we stand for.

Again, I have suggestions: Meredith Willson, George Washington Carver, and Lou Henry Hoover.

Meredith Willson, of course, was Iowa's *Music Man*. His work, ranging from *76 Trombones* to the *Iowa Fight Song*, not only brought a smile to your face, but tears to your eyes. During his career, he played with John Philip Sousa and wrote for the Beatles (*Till There Was You*). Perhaps with Grant Wood, Willson captured Iowa's spirit as well as anyone ever has.

Kidnapped as an infant by Confederates, George Washington Carver was the first black graduate student and professor at the Iowa State College of Agriculture and Mechanic Arts. Through his "chemurgy" work with peanuts and other plants, he helped invent the food processing industry. In a state valuing agriculture and inclusion, Carver would set an outstanding example for our children.

While Herbert Hoover's name graces many buildings, his wife, Lou, is less remembered. It was her humanitarian work with Herbert, though, that was perhaps the Hoovers' greatest legacy, saving millions from starvation in Europe and Asia. While Herbert was famously elected president, she preceded him in that position, as national president of the Girl Scouts.

Driving south into Mid-Prairie, the last school you pass is named for Irving Weber, an athlete, historian and Iowa City institution who contributed to his community well into his tenth decade. If putting Mr. Weber's name on the building justifies teaching kids about sportsmanship, civics and aging gracefully, it can only be a good thing. The same could be true for those we might honor, and who in turn would honor us.

Twenty-five years after what might have been *Van Allen High School*, do I still have too much time on my hands?

Evidently—but that's OK. Perhaps alone, I enjoy thinking about how these names might sound: *Wellman Willson*, *Kalona Lou Hoover*, and (my favorite) *Washington Township Washington Carver*.

And maybe I'm just slow to surrender, but I still think *Van Allen High* sounds better than *West*.

WHAT'S AN AAA DISTRICT WORTH TO YOU?

Drive around the Mid-Prairie district, and you'll see "daudy houses" attached to many rural homes. These additions embody a philosophy that governed human families for tens of thousands of years—in exchange for parents successfully raising their children to adulthood, "children" watched over their parents in their older years.

However, this implicit contract is eroding. Many kids don't live in the same state as their parents, much less the same house. Moreover, in many cases, our intergenerational economic arrangement has been superseded by Social Security taxes for the kids, and monthly checks for mom and dad.

Within our lifetimes, though, the greatest threat to older Americans may be the absence of any "kids" at all. Already, a demographic drought has engulfed the industrialized world. Specifically, fewer kids are being born than there are parents producing them.

According to the United Nations, there were 49 countries in 1997 in which the birthrate was lower than the replenishment rate—2.1 children per couple. Italy "led" the pack with 1.24 children per family, followed by Spain at 1.27 and Germany at 1.30. Even the United States is losing ground at 2.05.

If anyone thinks this is "someone else's problem," think again. According to the 2000 census, Iowa's children represent 24.6 percent of our population, the lowest number ever.

Since 1990, 63 of Iowa's 99 counties have lost kids; Cherokee led our pack with a 16.1 percent freefall. In terms of schools, 262 of Iowa's 374 districts lost enrollment this year, with 54 districts losing 5 percent and 5 losing 10 percent or more—in one year!

Mid-Prairie has remained remarkably stable, with budgeted enrollments of 1,243 in 1990 and 1,244 in 2000. However, our projected classroom students are dropping from 1,178 this year to 1,147 next, which means we're in the same sinking lifeboat as most everyone else (the difference between budgeted and classroom kids in another column).

Already, serious trial balloons suggest slashing our 99 counties by two-thirds. Those who think there will be 374 school districts in 2010 have helium in their heads.

How do you defeat the birth dearth? Mathematically, you have two options. Either have more kids yourself, or attract other folks' kids to your district.

There's nothing like a "can-do" spirit, but according to the UN, white American mothers average 1.6 kids each. Given that Mid-Prairie is overwhelmingly white (African Americans and Asians living in Kalona or Wellman can literally be counted on one hand—or less), that means we're not likely to replace ourselves.

That means attracting someone else's kids—and the one ethnicity that is exploding, even in Iowa, is our Hispanic population. Differing language and customs may make some queasy, but according to sociologist Amitai Etzioni, 89 percent of Hispanic parents agree that "to graduate from high school, students should be required to understand the common history and ideas that tie all Americans together."

If that sits well (and it should), and we want to ensure the long-term vitality of our community (as we should), we should also note Etzioni found that more than 80 percent of Hispanic parents believe it is "extremely important" to spend tax dollars on "educational opportunities for children." In other words, almost all parents share a common goal for their progeny—to be prepared to fully participate in our American society.

In truth, the Hispanic data mirror those found among the moneyed class. According to *Time* magazine, Standard and Poor's is analyzing school districts for student achievement, learning environment, finances, return on resources, fiscal outlook and demographic indicators. The financial ratings firm wants to provide information to "businesses that are considering different towns in which they might open a factory or an office. Such businesses know that the quality of schools is a major consideration for most employees."

You'll never find a daudy house on Wall Street, but an AAA rating for Mid-Prairie would represent the best community-wide ticket to our mutual financial security we'll ever see.

"Our" kids are not only our future, but in a real sense, our present. Whether we support them out of unconditional love or out-and-out selfishness, we would be well advised to ensure that every child is as welcome, and as well educated, as possible.

DNA OF SCHOOL CHOICE

A century from now, our descendants will look back upon 2000 as we did 1900 this year. Our peculiar presidential campaign will likely be a historical footnote. Instead, in 2100 they'll teach that "Y2K" was the year the human genome was decoded—with lessons not only applicable to our DNA, but to our ABCs.

A quick history lesson. In 1990, the U.S. and British governments tackled the genome project, expecting to work until 2005. According to Nobel economics laureate Gary Becker, "On the surface, one large, collaborative official effort made sense, since it could . . . avoid the duplication of effort and lack of coordination that would result from competing programs."

In 1998, a firm called *Celera* entered the race. Becker writes, "Celera's speedier progress seemed to light a fire under the government's program. . . . By speeding up the process to understand the genetic code—the essence of 'life'—by several years, competition from Celera may save thousands of lives through earlier discoveries of ways to prevent and treat deadly diseases."

Change a few words, and the same statements might apply to our public schools. Their staunchest supporters suggest one system "avoids(s) the duplication . . . that would result from competing programs," while market-oriented observers contend competition could restore the global preeminence our schools enjoyed a century ago. Joe Lieberman (before being tabbed as Al Gore's running mate) wrote, for example, "Our greatest challenge is to break through the gridlock on this issue and build the popular support necessary to make school choice a national priority."

As a Mid-Prairie board member, it's my job to help our schools be their best—but as with the presidential election, I have mixed feelings regarding the best choice to make. While I'm a free marketer at heart, my experience with unfettered free enterprise feeds my doubts when it comes to its applicability to our schools.

For example, one recent morning I settled for a raincheck instead of an advertised item at one store, and then was overcharged for another item at a second store. After pointing out the $1.50 error, I waited ten minutes for a surly salesperson to confirm my price, and then was forced to fill out a form that allowed them to fix their mistake.

A third store had a broken laminating machine—but could do the work on a second unit at twice the regular price. I then bought enough food at a grocery store to qualify for some free potatoes that, of course, they didn't have in stock. (I was told, "Come back tonight. We might have more then.")

Finally, I pulled into an empty fast food drive-through lane. After waiting several minutes, I heard "Wait a minute, I'll be with you soon." Two full minutes later, I drove off—unsatisfied in more ways than one.

Each of these enterprises is probably profitable, but on that day, they were no credit to capitalism. While I can afford to miss a few meals, our kids don't have that luxury when it comes to their educations. If some future school-for-hire decides to skimp on its service, our kids can't come back for a refund or raincheck. This is their one shot at learning.

Ready or not, the debate over "school choice" is one that will soon be engaged. As we swear in George W. Bush as our new president, and as we push for more teacher pay in return for more "accountability," this will no longer be an "academic" issue, but one with real implications for our schools and our society at large.

It's in that vein that I hope we arrive at a political and educational middle ground. If we can energize our schools with entrepreneurial attitudes, but administer them through public corporations that always put student needs and community aspirations before shareholder returns, we will all end up as winners. If we fail that test, as our government was doing with the human genome project, perhaps we deserve to lose.

As with our effort to decode the genome, the fate of our next generation rests, in part, on the way we structure and support public education. Let's hope that in 2100, our great-great grandchildren look back and applaud us for making the right decisions.

WHAT SHADE OF PURPLE CHEESE?

This week, a 15-year-old Ukrainian exchange student moves into our house for the next four months. While I may be not be an impartial judge, I'd like to think she's already one of Mid-Prairie's most important students.

What Tanya Vasilivna Ivanovich brings us is more than a stellar academic record and a superb command of English. She also represents a rare opportunity for our students and staff to interact with someone literally from the other side of the planet.

"Rare" is a word I use with caution, but at least on a statewide basis, the numbers back me up. Iowa State just released a poll of 3,049 Iowa farmers. ISU found that 63 percent had never worked—or even participated in recreational activities with—a member of any minority group.

That level of isolation has real costs, not only culturally, but in dollars and cents. Thomas Friedman, author of *The Lexus and the Olive Tree*, writes that when it comes to interaction across political, ethnic and especially international boundaries, every society has a choice. We can either run with the global economy "and live by its rules, or run alone . . . but accept the fact that you are going to have less access to capital, less access to technology and ultimately a lower standard of living for young people."

Running our lives by the global "rules" may seem like fighting words to those of us who cherish traditional small-town lifestyles, but in fact, the modern Internet-enabled economy may be what saves towns like ours from eroding into irrelevance.

A century ago, small towns thrived since farmers could only travel a half-day away by horse to get to market. Drive down Highway 22 and every eight miles you'll run into a new town—Nichols, Lone Tree, Riverside, Kalona, Wellman and Kinross.

Since the advent of the automobile, though, urban areas have been winning the demographic war. Last year, two-thirds of Iowa school districts lost students, a trend that can't continue long if small towns want to keep their schools—and communities—alive.

Fortunately, there is a solution to long-term economic survival, and it lies in education. If we can prepare our children to work with the billions of people who make up the potential worldwide markets for our local goods and services, our kids can live—and raise their families—wherever they want. Friedman quotes Klaus Schwab of the Davos World Economic Forum, who observed "We have moved from a world where the big eat the small to a world where the fast eat the slow."

That's where Tanya fits in, and any students or staff who look, speak or even think differently than the norm. By working and playing with them, our kids can learn to appreciate—and become competent at interacting with—the vast majority of the world's people who live outside our district's boundaries.

The rewards of cross-cultural fluency are enormous. Consider another rural area of the world—northern Italy. While not dotted with huge cities or blessed with rich natural resources, it is the most prosperous region in Europe—primarily because its residents know how to work with people who have backgrounds, tastes and interests different from their own.

An American ambassador to Italy once explained to Friedman, "Let's say you come to France, Germany and Italy and tell them, 'I want to buy some purple cheese.' What happens?

"Well, the French will tell you, 'Monsieur, cheese is never purple.' The Germans will tell you, 'Purple cheese is not in the catalog this year.' But the Italians . . . will say to you, 'What shade of purple would you like? Magenta?'"

Every time a Mid-Prairie student or staff member has the opportunity to interact with someone raised on a different continent, or even in a different community, it's another step toward learning our world isn't just black and white. It also comes in magenta, and every other color in our planetary paintbox.

Tanya Ivanovich will learn a great deal about America, and the hundreds of fascinating local folks she'll meet over this school year. If we keep our eyes and ears open, we'll learn just as much about her country and customs. If we keep our minds open, we'll learn even more about ourselves.

Welcome to Mid-Prairie, Tanya. It is our privilege to have you join our community.

SPEAK UP FOR FOREIGN LANGUAGES

This fall when I hit 40, I reconciled myself to the reality I will never win a marathon or dunk another volleyball (I never could dunk a basketball). Like it or not, most of us accept growing older with as much grace as we can muster.

When it comes to some learning, though, middle age doesn't arrive at 40—but at 14, if that old. For example, if you wait to learn a foreign language until puberty, chances are you'll never master it as well as an equally talented person who started just a few years earlier.

That's why a recent report by Iowa State University's Foreign Language Research Center is so important, and why I'm asking for ideas about how we can inject foreign language into our lower grades.

According to ISU, only one Iowa student in 10 attends an elementary school with a foreign language program—and the programs that do exist are described as "minimal" and "not very serious." Asked to comment, the Vilsack administration says it's focusing on class sizes and teacher quality, and that decisions to teach foreign languages are up to local school boards.

In Mid-Prairie, we're struggling to fund all-day everyday kindergarten, much less kiddie foreign language programs. But are such programs as "frilly" as they sound?

Consider the following. Five years ago, my kids (now 8 and 10) spent six months in Taiwan, my wife's homeland. They went from speaking mostly English to speaking all Chinese. My son Patrick graduated from a Taiwanese kindergarten, and when he returned to Alaska, he was initially placed in a bilingual education program.

Patrick is now an "enthusiastic" English speaker. Unfortunately, he's forgotten most of the Chinese he once knew, so he and his sister, Molly, spend every Sunday in an Iowa City "Chinese School" with similar kids, where they're soaking up the language like sponges.

When I compare their ease of learning with my efforts to muddle through Mandarin after marrying my wife, Jean, it's clear I should have started 20 years earlier, before my brain cells had set in cement. After two years of classes, I could converse with a patient Chinese speaker, but I've given up on hearing the "tones" in the language—which differentiate the "ma" that means "horse" from the "ma" that means "mother." (The hazards of such incompetence are obvious.)

It turns out that if you don't hear tones as a child, your brain may be incapable of hearing them as an adult. It's the same reason toddlers can learn second languages perfectly, but teenagers usually speak with accents the rest of their lives.

Many other countries begin teaching English earlier than we do our foreign languages. Jean started learning English in 7th grade, and Tanya, a Ukrainian exchange student in our home this fall, began practicing her ABCs in 2nd grade. From a darker perspective, Jean's parents were force-fed Japanese as children during the occupation of Taiwan before World War II. Today, 60 years later, they still speak Japanese fluently.

How do we inject foreign language into our elementary curriculum? A few ideas from my own experience. Because I switched grades at unusual times, I missed the whole "noun" and "verb" thing around 3rd grade—and didn't catch up until I took French in 9th. Through French, I understood why nouns and verbs were important. In third grade, had I learned about nouns and verbs in the context of English (which I "knew"), I doubt I would have cared about them much beyond the final worksheet.

Similarly, right now Molly is learning about "subjects" and "predicates." I taught the same thing to 3rd graders as a student teacher myself. Please keep this from Molly, but parsing subjects from predicates hardly ever comes up in real life. I'd rather we devote the time wasted on teaching linguistics to teaching a real language art, something that might be meaningful (and fun) to 8-year-olds (and maybe their teachers).

Mid-Prairie's formal goals call for "infusing" global education into our curriculum. Without new funds for language teachers, a conscious effort to integrate a foreign language into all parts of our curriculum—in the lower and upper grades—would be energy well spent. It would help our kids become competent in a second language, more appreciative and understanding of their first language, and learn there are other cultures in the world as interesting as their own.

If you have ideas about how we can accomplish this goal, let's talk. I'll have to do it in English, but if we do our jobs right, perhaps our kids will have more options a generation from now.

TAKE A DEEP BREATH

Schools are where you're supposed to go to find answers, but when it comes to school safety, lately that seems like an almost impossible task.

This week, the Mid-Prairie board received copies of the Wellman Elementary Crisis Plan. A generation ago, crises meant fires (walk outside in an orderly fashion) or tornadoes (hide under your desks). It's not that simple these days.

In addition to the traditional threats, Wellman's plan discusses toxic odors, bomb threats, explosions, suicides, and "imminent and immense" dangers to students and staff. Remember, this is an elementary school.

Unfortunately, the reality is our schools must prepare for "imminent and immense" dangers. It was just a year ago that 15 people died at Colorado's Columbine High School. Last month, we discovered "it can happen here" when a 15-year-old in a neighboring district was charged with terrorism and first-degree harassment for allegedly sending e-mails threatening that "friends will live, enemies will die."

Authorities are wrestling with the competing demands of ensuring school safety while trying to act compassionately with a student who is legally a child. Trying to provide guidance, the *Iowa City Press-Citizen* editorialized that "Just a few years ago, such threats would be handled with a stern talking to." According to the paper, "We all need to take a deep breath and remember that no one has been harmed. A potential threat was identified, and its implications are being explored. Beyond that, let's just wait to see what's learned. Don't overreact."

What's "overreact"? For three years, I managed the ACT Test Administration Department. During that time, there were deadly shootings at several of "our" schools. Instead of being mere abstractions in the newspaper, I had to worry about the teachers and counselors giving our tests and, of course, the kids who lost brothers, sisters and friends to the violence. It's hard not to "overreact."

I'm not the only one struggling. Last week, the Secret Service National Threat Assessment Center shared early results from a 20-year study of school shootings. According to *USA Today*, the study found "Students who are prone to violence tend not to make explicit threats but do communicate their intent to peers. They consistently keep adults out of the loop. And like political assassins, there is no single profile of a school shooter."

Robert Fein, a Secret Service psychologist, put the issue in terms the average parent or principal could understand when he wondered, "How can we deal with the fears that people have, and distinguish between 'We've got this situation we really ought to be concerned about,' and 'This kid is dressing funny.'"

Mid-Prairie is in the fortunate position of not having its own police force. That's not true for Indianapolis, where the "Chief of School Police" Jack Martin commented, "When you're talking about the difference between making a threat and posing a threat, school officials have a hard time making that distinction. Therefore, everything becomes important."

Everything? Apparently. The same day's newspaper reported four New Jersey kindergartners were suspended three days "for pointing fingers at each other as mock guns in an apparent game of cops and robbers." The assistant superintendent for the school district said "We're being beat up big time for this," but "I'm going to take the more conservative view and avoid a catastrophe rather than have a tragedy."

Suspending 6-year-olds for pointing fingers at each other seems laughable until you remember back just weeks ago, when a 6-year-old shot and killed a classmate in Michigan. Not funny any more.

Unlike some of what we teach in school, I hope the Wellman Elementary Crisis Plan represents learning that never has to be put to use in real life. Nonetheless, we better study hard. There may be no more important subject.

FASHION YOUR OWN OPINION

No one has ever accused me of being a fashion fanatic, so I suppose it shouldn't be surprising that this month I was well into my second day at a Louisiana high school before I noticed every student along one wall was wearing white khaki pants.

When I went to high school, the same observation could have been made about blue jeans, but khakis? No way. In the 1970s, our style was long hair and leisure suits.

I was in Lafayette to administer tests for my employer, ACT. During testing, the kids worked hard, but my job was easy—for the most part, I just stared at the students until time was up.

Bearing down with all my powers of observation, I noticed the class's khakis came in three colors—white, tan and blue. The shirts were also all earth tones—green, black, blue, brown or red—with not a stripe, logo or polka dot to be found.

Either these kids had a collective cool, or larger forces were at work. After testing, I asked what was up, and the answer came in a chorus—IT'S THE DRESS CODE!

The students patiently explained the rules to me. Pants must be khaki, and shirts must be in the solid colors listed above. A stripe along a collar is a violation, as are logos larger than a quarter. Everyone (staff included) had to wear a school lanyard with his or her ID hanging from it—and the boys couldn't have hair below their ears (although spiked and dyed hair were obviously OK).

While the next set of students tested, I imagined what these rules might mean in my house. To my 5th-grade son, clothes simply prevent knees from being skinned. For my 3rd-grade daughter, though, every day offers another chance to express her personal style, which is as "fashion-forward" as an 8-year-old can muster.

When the Louisiana class finished their explanation, I asked what they thought of the code. I expected passionate complaints, but the protests were pro forma at best—as in "What can we do? I guess it's OK."

In the next class, I noticed a few minor-league malefactors. One boy's shirt was untucked, a violation of the reminder posted on the door of a no-nonsense teacher: "SHIRTS TUCKED. ID'S ON. THIS IS YOUR LAST WARNING."

One girl had embroidered butterflies on her pant pockets, a breach for which she had yet to be "busted." Another traded her school lanyard for a fuzzy leopard-print substitute. Civil disobedience with style—now that's cool.

Later, I asked a teacher about the dress code. She said when it was adopted several years ago, students howled in agony, but parents loved having their kids focusing on the real priority of school, education.

She said within a year, her daughter grew fond of the rules. Instead of fretting over daily fashion decisions, she simply put on fresh clothes, secure in the knowledge that every other kid would be dressed about the same way. She added that every local district has since laid down the fashion law, all the way down to kindergarten, and none regrets its decision.

According to another teacher, "When you go to work, you dress for it. This is our kids' work. They should dress for it. It reminds them why they're here."

Despite the code, these kids are still as individual as our own. The only difference is that they've been mercifully excused from the fashion arms race. As an outsider, I couldn't tell whose families had money or which kids were on the academic fast track. They all looked like responsible young men and women, and perhaps because of it, they acted in kind.

I have not heard a drumbeat for a Mid-Prairie dress code and, as someone whose shirt was never tucked during high school, I can hardly believe I'm writing favorably of such a notion.

Perhaps we're all happy with the way we do things, but after five days in Cajun country, it's fair to say I'm less comfortable with our laissez-faire attitude than when I left.

SALUTING MILITARY INTELLIGENCE

Imagine a child who has attended 10 schools in as many years and whose father is sometimes absent six months at a stretch. There's a better-than-average chance this kid is black or Hispanic, and the odds are 50–50 he qualifies for free or reduced-price lunches.

This seems like a surefire recipe for educational disaster. But the surprising truth is there are more than 100,000 American children who could be described by the first paragraph and, as a whole, they are doing better than their peers in conventional schools.

The children attend one of 226 schools operated by the U.S. Department of Defense. In a Vanderbilt University study, researchers found these sons and daughters of soldiers outranked most of their civilian counterparts on the 1998 National Assessment of Educational Progress. As reported in *USA Today*, "White, black and Hispanic students in DOD schools each scored well compared with peers in other states, and the performance gap between the races was narrower than in the public schools."

Why the stellar showing? It's not because they're the offspring of hard-charging officers. About 94 percent are children of enlisted personnel, 35 percent change schools each year, and 50 percent qualify for free or reduced lunches.

Success apparently comes from doing a few things exceptionally well. First, parents are involved in the schools. According to the newspaper, "Soldiers are instructed that their 'place of duty' is at their child's school on parent-teacher conference day, and are given time off to volunteer at school each month."

Other key factors are teachers who consistently teach within their fields, smaller schools and—in a finding that's sure to rub some independent Iowans the wrong way—"Each school's curriculum is about the same, based on set standards of what students should know. . . . Students are tested frequently, and the results are used in headquarters to give principals detailed analyses of student performance. The schools, in turn, identify student improvement needs and set learning goals."

Like DOD schools, Mid-Prairie enjoys extensive parental participation. Parent-teacher conference attendance rates are 95 percent-plus at our elementary schools, and the legions serving in our classrooms bring new meaning to the term *volunteer army.*

Like every other Iowa district, though, Mid-Prairie operates without statewide academic standards. Alone among the 50 states, Iowa has determined such standards are best set at the local level—and, according to the *Des Moines Register*, succeeded in persuading the U.S. Congress that we alone should be exempted from full participation in the so-called *Leave No Child Behind Act* signed by President Bush last week.

There's little doubt that it's easier for an intelligent and free-thinking faculty to love one's own creation than a dictate from on high. Even at Mid-Prairie, though, we formally examine each discipline only once every seven years, so many newer faculty members haven't participated in creating the official curriculum they teach.

Moreover, if they are anything like me, once they've grown accomplished in teaching to a particular program, it becomes hard to justify the time, energy and risks inherent in radically reworking the curriculum.

Even if we succeed in developing top-notch homegrown goals, that doesn't help the child who moves to Mid-Prairie from another district with its own unique goals. Those newcomers, like kids who might move from Mid-Prairie someday, will be forced to pick up in a new system where they are ahead in some areas, behind in others—and swimming against the tide overall. If the academic undercurrents are strong enough, it's no wonder some kids "drown."

Anyone who knows me knows I treasure saying what I think, even if I'm the only one who thinks it. Still, when I ponder 371 Iowa school districts regularly reinventing a similar wheel, I can't help but wonder if that time and talent couldn't be put to better use actually teaching kids a more standard—and yes, even a "cookie-cutter"—curriculum.

A uniform curriculum apparently works well for the children of our men and women in uniform. As Iowa examines the way it conducts its academic affairs in a results-oriented and economically challenging environment, it may be time to run this idea up the flagpole and see if anyone salutes.

GUTS AND GRACE

No matter which direction you travel from Mid-Prairie these days, it seems you're likely to encounter an educational embarrassment.

Case 1—Iowa's men's basketball team. After weeks of uninspired performance on the court and none in the classroom, Reggie Evans was benched for the Ohio State game, as were the other regular starters. Iowa lost, but for the first time in too long, most fans felt proud to call themselves Hawkeyes.

Case 2—Iowa City's high schools. Just a few miles down the road, basketball fans from City High hurled sexual insults, and waved dollar bills, at West's dance team. No one stepped forward to stop the nastiness. This time, few felt proud to be a Little Hawk or Trojan.

Case 3—the Piper, Kansas, school board. When 28 sophomores plagiarized papers from the Internet, their teacher—consistent with district policy—gave them no credit for the assignment, which resulted in them failing their class. Buckling to parental pressure, the board overruled the teacher, her principal and their principles, allowing the kids to pass. Reportedly "whooping and hollering," the students told their teacher, "We don't have to listen to you anymore." They were right. She's quit in disgust.

Cases 4 and more—too many episodes, for my comfort, involving me.

Last fall, I attended a football game involving our favorite high school team. I sat in a student-dominated section where most words I heard seemed to have four letters. I'm hard to offend, but those kids succeeded. I can't help but wonder how it impressed the gentleman on my left, who grew up in an era when fans wore suits to games, or the two children to my right—who wondered why Dad didn't tell the hooligans to knock it off.

The truth is, it was easier to let it slide. As a result, I spent several hours unsuccessfully ignoring the crudeness around me and the cowardice within me. More important, students who should have been reminded that society frowns upon boorish banter failed to receive not only the lesson they deserved, but one that they needed.

Iowa coach Steve Alford also knows the queasiness that comes from taking the easy way out. Before the benching, Alford confessed he'd "had a feeling in my stomach that I haven't liked." After the game he said, "We lost the game today, but if we've got to lose, that's the way I like to lose."

It's not often a Big 10 coach utters the phrase, "That's the way I like to lose," and Jim O'Brien noticed. "For him to demonstrate courage by doing what he thinks is the right thing, and not playing their best player in a game such as this, is a credit to him and his staff," said the OSU coach. "I guarantee you that is not an easy decision to make."

Anyone who disagreed should have been silenced by Rod Thompson. The "citizen-senior" scored 15 points during the game and more afterwards when he stated, "We can't let a star not go to class. Who knows, a kid coming here who might be a star, he's like, 'I didn't see Reggie going to class so I don't have to go to classes.' It's really good to nip that in the bud."

Iowa City's principals are being hammered because they didn't halt the dollar waving directed at West's dancers. They should have, but there were hundreds of other potential authority figures present that could have slowed down the stupidity, but like me, let it slide.

Colin Powell tells of growing up in a neighborhood where news of his shortcomings reached his parents faster than he could run home from his mischief. With his neighbor's "help," Powell learned right from wrong. Had Colin's elders "minded their own business," Powell wonders if he'd be Secretary of State today.

If there was a future cabinet officer in our crowd, I didn't help that kid learn how leaders behave—by my words or example. It's easy to complain about ethical lapses from a distance. Up close, it isn't so simple.

Next time I see you in the stands, let's hope we have a family-friendly atmosphere. If we aren't so lucky, let's also hope we have the guts and the grace to do something about it.

Chapter Eleven

We Have That Chance

The first time I remember Lyndon Johnson was during his visit to the Herbert Hoover Presidential Library. LBJ wanted to build a similar monument to himself, and went to West Branch for ideas.

While I remember (I think) shaking his hand, I've only just discovered his greatest monument—a 1965 speech titled *The American Promise*. Imagine squinting at a grainy black-and-white TV, and hearing President Johnson speak these words: "Dignity cannot be found in a man's possessions. It cannot be found in his power, or in his position. It really rests on his right to be treated as a man equal in opportunity to all others."

The immediate issue was the Voting Rights Act. For Johnson, what made the question so compelling were his experiences as a teacher.

> My first job after college was as a teacher in Cotulla, Texas, in a small Mexican-American school. Few of them could speak English, and I couldn't speak much Spanish.
>
> My students were poor and they often came to class without breakfast, hungry. They knew even in their youth the pain of prejudice. They never seemed to know why people disliked them. But they knew it was so, because I saw it in their eyes.
>
> I often walked home late in the afternoon, after the classes were finished, wishing there was more that I could do. But all I knew was to teach them the little that I knew, hoping that it might help them against the hardships that lay ahead. . . .
>
> I never thought then, in 1928, that I would be standing here in 1965. It never even occurred to me in my fondest dreams that I might have the chance to help the sons and daughters of those students, and to help people like them all over this country.

But now I do have that chance—and I'll let you in on a secret—I mean to use it. And I hope that you will use it with me.

During the 13 years I spent in Alaska, my friends knew two things about Iowa—corn and schools. Iowa was—and is—the best at both. Our reputation not only gives us prestige, but power. If we live up to our promise, in both senses of the word, we can set the educational standard for America. And, while this may sound as boastful as LBJ, I'm convinced Mid-Prairie has the student, staff and community vision to set the bar for Iowa.

Mid-Prairie High School went a long way towards proving that this year when it was the only Iowa high school to win a First In the Nation in Education (FINE) Award. We may not win every year, or most years, but I'm hard-pressed to believe there's anyone, anywhere, with whom we should hesitate to compare our efforts.

External evaluators may look to hard data for excellence, but for me, the evidence is as obvious—and invisible—as the air we breathe. The best example was this year's MPHS graduation, probably the 20th such ceremony in which I've participated. While each was special, I've never attended an event in which pride, satisfaction and even love so suffused the room.

It wasn't because MPHS won an academic award, or a basketball championship, that folks felt as they did. It was because so many people in the room had worked as if on a mission—and rejoiced that their efforts had successfully prepared 78 young people to meet life's next challenges.

This is the last column I'll write during my three-year term on the school board. Agree or disagree with what I've written, I hope you've been prompted to consider the role education plays in our society. I'm no philosopher, but I know a good quote when I see one. Said the Greek poet Heraditus: "The soul is dyed the color of its thoughts. Think only on those things that are in line with your principles and can be seen in the full light of day. The content of your character is your choice. Day by day, what you choose, what you think, and what you do is what you become."

Mid-Prairie has become an extraordinary school district. As a community, we can create the best district in what I believe is the best state in the best country in the world, and by our example, lead others on similar paths to educational excellence.

As President Johnson said, given that opportunity, "I'll let you in on a secret—I mean to use it. And I hope that you will use it with me."

About the Author

Jim Hussey was born in Iowa and educated in its public schools before heading out of state to earn degrees in economics, political science, journalism and higher education. He first worked as a reporter in Alaska, and then as a faculty member and administrator in the University of Alaska system. After 13 years in Alaska, he returned to Iowa in 1996, where he continues to work in education. Jim was elected to the Mid-Prairie Community School District Board of Directors in 1999. He and his wife, Jean, have two children who attend the Mid-Prairie schools.